FOOD &
FOLKLORE

A Year of Italian Festivals

LISA M. VOGELE

DEDICATION

In memory of

Pauline Olenoski Wisniewski
&
Michael Santos Alicea

8-2016

ISBN: 0692722432
ISBN-13: 978-0692722435

CONTENTS

ACKNOWLEDGMENTS

Thank you to my husband Mark for his support and patience while working on this book and for marrying me in Siena, Italy. To my mother Laura for introducing me to her Italian friends. Mo, Judi, B, Kathleen, Molly, Joan, Amy, Lois, Tom, Carol, Rene, Candy, Dasha, Aimee, Monika, Cousin Liz, and Marco Poverino for their encouragement.

Kathleen & Sebastian for sharing my first Italian festival experience. Carolyn & Cyndi for traveling with me on that first trip to Italy years ago. Ann & Robin for my last trip to Italy. Thanks to all of you for letting me plan and coordinate the highlights of our travel time together.

To my Italian friends that make my trips so special: Viviana (Leopolda), Andrea, Fernanda, Elena, Paola D., Paola V., Marco, Kerry, Franco and Silvia in Bologna (and Vado). Bianca, Martina, Christian, Andrea and the crew at Cattivi Frati of Buonconvento in Tuscany.

Special thanks to: Ad for the cover design; my Italian instructor Lucia; the editing and self-publishing advice given by Ann McGough, Bernice Alicea, Michael Conniff and Donna Davis.

Thank you to family and friends for letting me go on and on about Italy all of these years.

Map of Italy and Italian Regions

Whenever I go anywhere but Italy for vacation, it always feels as if I have made a mistake – Erica Jong.

INTRODUCTION

In August of 2009 I crossed an item off my bucket list: two weeks of Italian lessons in Florence at *Scuola Leonardo da Vinci*. Fortunately for me, two of my friends were also in Florence at the time on a round-the-world trip. We only had two days of overlap for sightseeing before my classes started and decided to rent a car for a whirlwind circle trip with an overnight in Montepulciano. After unpacking we checked out the town and noticed some flyers posted advertising a local festival. We saw a line forming with someone collecting money and joined in.

It was one of the *quartiere* (neighborhood) meals and we were the only *stranieri* (foreigners) there. The quartiere had a mobile kitchen setup in a small courtyard with a group of Italian grandmothers cooking away. We feasted on some *bucatini al cinghiale* then needed to walk it off. We thought that was all there was to the festival, but that is when things really started to get exciting... the beat of the drums, the flag throwers, the costumed medieval court of each neighborhood on parade ... that's when my addiction to festival travel began.

Each trip abroad since has been accompanied by research into what is going on locally, particularly festivals. Even though websites and apps exist for festival finding, I found them to be a little cumbersome, not updated and lacking some basic information. I decided to write a book so that I could share my passion for these experiences with people looking to do something a little different. I have been to Italy more times than any other country outside of the United States. Because I have *been there and done that* when it comes to some of the major tourist sites, incorporating these events pushed me further into areas of this beautiful country I may not have visited.

This guide is intended to provide you with the tools and tips necessary to incorporate local festivals into your travel planning. Whether you have been to Italy before or not, festivals are a great way to sample authentic cuisine and get more local. This is not a comprehensive guide of every festival in existence and I am sure someone may be offended if their favorite isn't included. My apologies in advance.

Over 450 festivals are included in this guide. I am sharing my personal research and "travel notes" with you. There are all kinds of festivals to explore whether you're a foodie, history buff or oenophile. My primary focus is on food & folklore at non-religious events with a few wine festivals thrown in. In Italy, every day has a patron saint and the potential for a festival in their honor. On occasion, I may list a festival that has strong religious connotations because the food, wine, and/or folklore associated with the event is steeped in a greater historical context or cuisine. I would have had encyclopedias full of festivals if I had tried to include *every* religious festival.

Tasting food made by locals for locals, seeing a medieval re-enactment if you're a history buff, hearing the medieval drumbeat if you love live musical entertainment—these are memorable and unique experiences you can have by attending the festivals included in this book—or finding some new ones.

Buona fortuna!

NOTES

If you can't live longer, live deeper – Italian Proverb

1

THE MAGIC OF FESTIVALS

On the eve of my first trip to Italy in 1999 my work colleague Dana gave me some vacation advice: "stay in the present moment." He knew I had been planning and researching my heart out to create a spectacular vacation experience for me and my girlfriends. I have been employing that advice on vacations ever since; and in fact, it is this advice that transforms simply attending a festival into magical moments for me.

Festivals with historical reenactments are particularly easy to live in the moment and feel as though you have been magically transported back in time. Hearing a drumbeat from a far off corner of a town grow in volume as it gets closer and closer until you feel it in your bones. Watching the *sbandieratori* (flag throwers) display their amazing skills after hours of practice. Tasting the fabulous food and savoring every single bite. Sitting amongst local residents carrying on their conversations in a language or dialect different from your own. The sporting skills of an archery competition or traditional race. The visual feast of costumed participants that are in character re-enacting a legendary event.

Slow down. Open your eyes, ears, taste buds, and you too will experience these magical moments that can enhance your vacation and create special memories you will hold in your heart. The ordinary will become extraordinary.

Italy is always a good idea. – Unknown

2

PLANNING YOUR EXPERIENCE

Festival dates/weekends can change from year to year depending on how the month falls on specific calendar days. Sometimes smaller to mid-size festivals aren't announced formally until a few months ahead of the event, and this can make planning around them a little tricky. Dates included in this book anticipate the typical dates and weekends the festivals are held each year but should be confirmed. For example, on my last research trip for this guide, a very well-known festival in the Cinque Terre area of Liguria changed from its typical weekend because there were five Saturdays instead of four, because of the way the calendar dates fell that particular month.

Remember these festivals are predominantly held by locals, for locals, so they could be canceled or rescheduled for a variety of reasons ahead of time or at the last minute (such as weather).

How this Book is Organized

Italy is divided into twenty regions. The regions are broken up into smaller provinces, then cities or towns. Each region of Italy has a dedicated chapter that includes: a brief overview of the region, a detailed description of one regional festival, and a listing of suggested regional festivals throughout the year. Each chapter title/region is listed in Italian and English.

How to Use this Book

If you are already planning a trip to Italy and have your plans outlined then use this book and its cross-references to look for which festivals are happening in the region and dates you will be there. If you have a favorite food or snack, then look through the food cross-reference to see if we have suggested a festival focusing on that food type (such as chocolate or cheese). If you'd like to hit as many as possible then focus on festival listings in May, August, September, and October which are the most popular festival months. If costumes, floats, and parades are your passion, plan to go during carnival time (usually in February) and enjoy the revelry.

How to Research

The Internet is obviously your best resource for planning to attend some festivals. It helps to *search using Italian words and phrases* — then click on the language of your choice or use a translation site (such as translate.google.com) to assist you with reading the information. A glossary of key words has been included at the rear of this book to assist you with determining what keywords to use. Here are three scenarios describing search strategies:

1. *Festivals in Specific Locations*. Use official tourism websites such as www.italy.com and the links to the different regions and provinces it provides. For example, if you are going to Abruzzo, search on *"turismo ufficiale Abruzzo."* The official tourism sites often keep a calendar of events that will list the festivals for their region or province. If you know the town you will visit, use the term "pro loco" for the local promotional board, for example: *"Sulmona Abruzzo Pro Loco"* if you are going to be visiting Sulmona in Abruzzo.

2. *Keyword search*. Use this method if you are looking for a specific type of festival and/or at a specific time. For instance, you love artichokes and you plan to be in Italy in May, but you are not sure which regions you plan to visit yet. Search on *"Maggio carciofi sagra."* (see Glossary & Keyword section for a more comprehensive list of useful Italian festival terms)

3. *Specialty Websites and Apps*. Festival-specific websites and apps: Using broader terms such as *"Festa Italia"* or *"Sagra Italia"* will bring up different websites that report on festivals from time to time or regularly list what is occurring. The issue I have found with these is that the database grows and festivals are not always removed when they no longer exist or modified once a town decides to hold it at a different time of year. They are very helpful for ideas but make sure you confirm whatever information you find through further research.

Confirm Confirm Confirm

Bookmark the website for your festival or the tourism website and check back periodically. If it involves an event to which you bought a ticket, you still need to confirm since certain events could be delayed in the case of rain or inclement weather.

Parking

Parking can be the hardest part of attending a festival. Expect to walk some distance and wear comfortable shoes. If you are attending a long-standing, annual event, consider staying in the town. You will already be there for the festival and can use it as a home base for day trips. If someone in your party has an ailment with limited mobility, drop them off as close as you can; sometimes spaces are reserved for the handicapped but if you are travelling, you may not have the appropriate hang tag or sticker.

Tickets

If the festival you are attending requires tickets for entry or assigned seating (example: *Calcio Storico Fiorentino* in Florence) ensure you know when tickets go on sale and set an alarm on your phone remembering which time zone you are in and which time zone Italy is in (Greenwich Mean Time +1 or +2 hours depending on whether it is summer or not; typically 6 hours ahead of Eastern Time in the United States).

At the Festival

The food festivals typically follow the same pattern: look for the food stand or tent, stand in the food ordering line, when it's your turn you order your food, the order-taker writes your order and adds up your bill, you pay, take your ticket and find a seat at a communal table. A waiter will come by, take your ticket and deliver your food to you when it is ready.

There are variations of this basic order of business depending on whether there is a variety of foods, different foods in each neighborhood of a village or it's a historic festival with multiple food stands. In any case, look for the stand or stands with the foods you want, order, pay and wait. The food you get will be fresh, local and cheaper than you would pay sitting in a restaurant nearby.

What is a sagra?

The word *sagra* has multiple meanings in Italian. The dictionary meaning is strictly a church festival. However, while many may be associated with church functions, they are often held with the purpose of raising money for a local organization, charity or sports team. In this book, sagra means feast or festival whether it is church-related or not. You may see *sagra* and *sagre* used throughout this book; *sagre* is the plural of *sagra*.

How to Read a Sagra Poster

If you are lucky enough to come upon a poster for a local *sagra* in your travels or through your research and you know the common elements, you will quickly gain an understanding of the key festival information. Posters range from smaller festivals with simple graphics and bright colors to long-standing events that draw visitors each year and have greater detail and fancier graphics. Two different Tuscan festival posters of varying scope and focus are included on the following pages to illustrate the types of information they provide.

Sample 1: Sagra del Fritto in Monteroni d'Arbia

This poster lists the specific days in May it is held (May 13, 14, 15, 20 & 21). The location of the festival (Piazza della Resistenza in Monteroni d'Arbia, south of Siena). Every night of the festival there is different entertainment. The food stands open at 7:00 P.M. each evening (*ore 19 apertura stands gastrononomic*). The *classic* menu focus for each night of this fried food festival is listed (fish on Fridays, veal on Saturdays and veal with brains on the single Sunday (*Domenica 15 maggio*).

Sample 2: Sagra del Cinghiale

This wild boar festival is being held for the 42nd time in Riparbella, near Pisa. The poster notes the time span of the festival (November 9-17) but in fact is held *only* on the Saturdays and Sundays that occur within that time frame. There is dinner and entertainment on the Saturday nights and special exhibitions with lunch and dinner on the Sundays.

In Italy, they add work and life on to food and wine

— *Robin Leach*

3

ABRUZZO

ABRUZZO

Abruzzo is a region of vast geographic differences, from snowcapped peaks to shoreline, and is home to three national parks, one regional park, and thirty-eight protected nature reserves. This region has trained and produced internationally known chefs, is home to 20 of the "Most Beautiful Villages in Italy,"(according to *I Borghi più belli d'Italia*) the birthplace of Ovid and the infamous snake festival of Cocullo.

When it comes to food, the main course dishes that are most popular depend on where you are in

Abruzzo - if along the coastline it will be a seafood stew or if in the mountains it will be a meat dish such as lamb roasted over an open fire on a stick (*arrosticini*). Sugar coated almonds, also known as "confetti" or "Jordan almonds," are popular throughout the world and often used as wedding favors. Almonds are a popular ingredient in other desserts made with dough, nougat or just the almonds themselves. If you've ever been to an Italian wedding, chances are you were greeted at your place setting with a small tulle bag of confetti; not the paper type, the almond type. Used to celebrate significant unions and births, the candy coated almond treats are used as a thank you to guests and come in many different colors, each with its own meaning. Casa Pelino has been making confetti in nearby Sulmona since 1783 but the family got their start in Introdacqua.

The typical pasta course may include *macheroni all chitarra, gnocchi carrati* or *pastuccia*. The *macheroni all chitarra* is made with pasta cut into strips (like guitar strings) and served with a lamb, pork or goose *ragu*. Gnocchi carrati is made with bacon, egg and sheep's-milk cheese. Pastuccia is a stew of polenta with sausage, egg and grated sheep's-milk cheese. This region is home to *L'aglio Rossa di Sulmona* (Sulmona red garlic) and the saffron fields of Navelli.

FESTIVAL FOCUS
Festa dei Serpari
Snake Festival of Cocullo
Cocullo

Every first of May starting at noon, Mass is held in the main square of Cocullo and snakes are laid upon the statue of San Domenico. San Domenico is honored during this feast for ridding the village of snakes in the 11th century and his statue, along with the snakes, is paraded through the town for about 1.5 hours, followed by fireworks. Stands are set up around town to feed the thousands that descend on this town in the hills west of Sulmona. There are four types of non-venomous snakes used in the procession. The snake handlers (*serpari*) start gathering the snakes in March for the celebration and when completed they release the snakes into the woods.

FESTIVALS OF ABRUZZO

January
Festa di Sant'Antonio Abate
Festival of Saint Anthony the Abbot
Collelongo

February
Chocofest
Chocolate Festival
Francavilla

March
La Festa dei Fuochi
The Feast of Fires
Sulmona

April
Carciofesta
Artichoke Festival
Cupello

Festa della Sfogliatella di Lama
The Lama Sfogliatella Party
Lama dei Peligni

May
Feste dei Banderesi
Festival of the Flagthrowers
Bucchianico

Festa dei Serpari
Snake Festival of Cocullo
Cocullo

Virtù Feast
Feast of the Virtues
Teramo

June
Lu Cencialone
Lu Cencialone
Silvi

Mese di Brodetto di Pesce Alla Vastese
Month of Fish Broth in Vasto
Vasto

July
Festa del tartufo
Truffle Festival
Campovalano di Campli

Sagra della Porchetta
Feast of Porchetta
Carpineto Sinello

Settimana del Mare
Week of the Sea
Giulianova Lido

Dieta Mediterranea
Mediterranean Food Festival
Marina di Pescara

Fiera della Pastorizia
Fair of the Sheep Farmers
Piano Roseto (Crognaleto)

Cala Lenta
Slow Cove Seafood Festival
San Vito Chietino

August
Sagra della Patata
Potato Festival
Barisciano

La Sagra del Prosciuto
The Festival of Prosciutto
Basciano

Estate a Calascio
Summer in Calascio
Calascio

Sagra della Porchetta Italica
Sagra della Porchetta Italica
Campli

Tacchinando Canzanese
Turkey Festival
Canzano

Rassegna Ovini
Sheep Festival
Castel del Monte

Sagra Paesana
Sagra Paesana
Introdacqua

La Perdonanza
The Pardon
L'Aquila

La Sagra delle Sagre
The Festival of Festivals
L'Aquila

Mostra dei Vini Tipici
Wine Exhibition Typical
Montepagano

Calici di Stelle
Goblets of Stars
Ortona

Festa del Ritorno
Feast of the Return
Vasto

September
Buon Gusto - Rassegna Formaggi d'Abruzzo
Good taste - Review of the Cheeses of Abruzzo
Gessopalena

October
Sagra delle Lenticchie di Santo Stefano di Sessanio
Feast of the Lentils of Santo Stefano di Sessanio
Santo Stefano di Sessanio

November
San Martino in Vino
San Martino in Wine
Bolognano

Festa del Ringraziamento
Thanksgiving
Introdacqua

December
La Notte dei Faugni
The Night of Bonfires
Atri

Festa di San Nicola da Bari e Sagra delle Fave
Feast of St. Nicholas of Bari and Feast of the Bean
Pollutri

Even now I miss Italy dearly, I dream about it every night.
– Eila Hiltunen

4

VALLE D'AOSTA

AOSTA VALLEY

The smallest region by both size and population, the Valle D'Aosta is home to three of the largest peaks in Europe: Monte Bianco (or Mont Blanc), Monte Cervino (or the Matterhorn), and Monte Rosa. The peaks are snow-capped year round and are stunningly beautiful. The Valle d'Aosta has been autonomous since 1948, after World War II, when it was separated from the Region of Piemonte. It has one province, Aosta, 74 towns and is bordered by Switzerland to the North and France to the West. The region has two official languages, Italian and French. The multi-cultural influences of its neighbors are felt in the cuisine and architecture. Thanks to the Mont Blanc Tunnel, it's only a 20 minute drive through to Chamonix in France.

Referred to as the "Rome of the Alps" because of its Roman ruins in an alpine mountain setting, it has excellent hiking in the summer and fall and skiing in the winter and early spring. Rome conquered the region in 25 BC from the local Salassi, a Celtic tribe, and called it *Augusta Praetoria Salassorum* (modern day Capital of Aosta) which evolved into Valle d'Aosta or Valley of Augustus.

Fontina cheese found in the Aosta Valley is not the same as other fontina cheeses produced in the United States or Scandinavia. The term Fontina is almost 700 years old and the cheese has a mild, buttery, nutty flavor that is perfect for melting and using for a fondue meal with vegetables and meat. Both the local fontina and *jambon de bosses* are PDO-designated by the European Union. *PDO* is the acronym for *Product of Designated Origin* and is used to protect the quality of authentic products. Other regional ingredients popular in food include: mushrooms, game, beef, blueberries, raspberries, chestnuts, apples, pears, honey and herbs.

FESTIVAL FOCUS
Fiera di Sant'Orso
Fair of the Bear
Aosta

There is more than skiing to draw you to the Aosta Valley. Aosta is an old Roman town in northwestern Italy with a dramatic mountain backdrop. Starting about the year 1000, the Fiera di Sant'Orso began with a local monk who distributed clothing and sabot (wooden shoes) to the poor. Today the tradition continues with over 1,000 artisans and stands distributed throughout the town for the entire final weekend of January.

Early morning until late at night on Saturday and Sunday artisans will display intricate wood carvings, sculptures, baskets, ceramics and other forms of fine and folk art. There is a food and wine tent showcasing every local delicacy you can imagine: cheese, meat, jams, wines and more. A specialty tent called *"L'Atelier"* has over 80 vendors selling a wide variety of clothing, furnishings and housewares.

At night, stroll the streets while sipping warm, mulled wine and listening to spontaneous folk music and singing. Participate in some local food tastings or buy a *grolla* and share it with friends. A grolla is essentially a friendship cup; it's carved out of wood, has 2, 4, 6 or 8 spouts and is intended to be filled with coffee, grappa and sugar. These can be seen in use during après ski and you can buy one from a wood artisan and take it home with you. It's the perfect souvenir to bring with you for your next party.

FESTIVALS OF THE AOSTA VALLEY

January
Fiera di Sant'Orso
Fair of the Bear Saint
Aosta

April
Festa Patronale di San Giorgio
Festival of Saint George
Hone

Bataille des Reines
Battle of the Queens
Multiple Towns

June
Festa patronale di San Giovanni
Patron Saint's Festival of St. John
Gressoney-Saint-Jean

July
Festa del Lardo of Arnad
Lard Festival of Arnad
Arnad

Festa del Pane Nero
Black Bread Festival
Champorcher

La Veillà
The Veilla
Cogne

Prosciutto crudo di Bosses
Prosciutto Festival
Saint-Rhémy-en-Bosses

Sagra della Seupa à la Vapelenentse
The Vapelenentse Soup Festival
Valpelline

August
Festa del Sargnun
The Sargnun Cheese Festival
Champorcher

September
Sagra della Fontina
Fontina Cheese Festival
Etroubles

October
Festa delle Mele
Apple Festival
Antey-Saint-André & Gressan

Bataille des Reines
Battle of the Queens
Aosta

Sagra del Miele di Châtillon
Festival of Chatillon Honey
Chatillon

Festa della Castagna
Festival of the Chestnut
Lillianes

For us to go into Italy and to penetrate into Italy is like a most fascinating act of self-discovery.– D.H. Lawrence

5

PUGLIA

APULIA

Looking at the outline for Italy, it is easy to identify Puglia's approximate geographical location as occupying the heel and cowboy boot spur in southeastern Italy, following the Adriatic coastline. Puglia is made up of six provinces: Bari, Barletta-Andria-Trani, Brindisi, Foggia, Lecce and Taranto. The region is very flat and is perhaps most famous for its *trulli*, the white cone shaped houses found predominantly in the Itria Valley and Alberobello.

Puglia is a large producer of wine. It used to be shipped off and blended with wines from other regions but is now also produced for local table consumption. Of the wines produced here, 82 percent is red and 18 is white.

Garlic is a dominant flavor to dishes in the province of Foggia but as you move further south onions dominate the flavoring. It is common to see fruits and vegetables drying outside of homes to prepare them for storage and later use. Almonds and olives also provide flavor to typical *Pugliese* dishes like the famous *"fichi mandorlati"* (*almondized* figs infused with spices).

Residents start their meals with fried breads stuffed with meats, cheeses or vegetables, tuna or salame. A popular shape of pasta here is *troccoli*, a long square noodle similar to the *Abruzzese* chitarra. Perhaps Puglia's most common pasta shape is the orecchiete shaped like little ears. While lamb, goat and veal are common it is no surprise that with many kilometers of coastline, seafood dishes have a place at the table. It is common to have a plate of raw vegetables for dessert here or melone, a very sweet watermelon-like native fruit to the region.

FESTIVAL FOCUS
Bacco nelle Gnostre
Bacchus in the Meeting Points
Noci

Music, dancing and vino fill the streets each year in Noci at the Feast of Bacchus. Named after Bacchus, the Roman god of wine and intoxication, this fall feast is held at the beginning of November. The smell of roasting chestnuts waft through the air and the sound of folklore and modern musical groups fills the night as patrons queue up for local food and new wine. You'll find yourself tapping your feet and moving to the music listening to the performers. It's a little bit of history, a bit of culture and a lot of food and wine.

FESTIVALS OF APULIA

February
Carnevale di Putignano
Carnival of Putignano
Putignano

May
Palio of Taranto
Palio of Taranto
Taranto

June
Festival of the Sea
Festival of the Sea
Taranto

July
Il Palio dei Capotosta
The Palio of Capotosta
Mola di Bari

Sagra del Polpo
Octopus Feast
Mola di Bari

Festa di Santa Domenica e la Notte delle Luci
Feast of Santa Domenica and the Night of the Lights
Scorrano

Sagra del Pesce
Fish Festival
Zapponeta

August
Citta dei Trulli Festival
City of Trulli Festival
Alberobello

Sagra della Focaccia
Feast of Focaccia
Cassano delle Murge

Sagra dell'Arrosto
Roast Festival
Martina Franca

Torneo dei Rioni
Tournament of the Districts
Oria

September
Sagra della Burrata
Festival of Burrata Cheese
Andria

November
Bacco nelle Gnostre
Bacchus in the Gnostre (Meeting Points)
Noci

December
Sagra della Porchetta e del Maiale
Festival of Porchetta and the Pig
Martina Franca

NOTES

What is the fatal charm of Italy? What do we find there that can be found nowhere else? I believe it is a certain permission to be human, which other places, other countries, lost long ago.
— Erica Jong

6

BASLICATA

BASILICATA

Basilicata feels more desolate and isolated than other parts of Italy because it is less dense by population and the landscape appears unforgiving. It was originally called Lucania and natives of the region are referred to as *Lucani*. A historically poor province, it was subject to massive emigration in the 20th century.

The most mountainous region of southern Italy, the only flat area is found along the coastline. Surprisingly, you can downhill ski on Monte Sirino in the winter even though this is one of the southernmost regions of Italy.

Centuries old, extraordinary cave dwellings called "*sassi*" distinguish the city of Matera. Connected by narrow paths and feeling like a maze, they were hollowed out of rock centuries ago to serve as homes. Matera is also home to "*chiese rupestri*," cave churches carved in the local stone.

Founded by the Greeks, conquered by Romans and under different foreign rule at times, many cultures have influenced the food here. Some believe that Basilicata is the birthplace of pasta. The region is known for Lucanian pecorino cheese, beans, sausage, olive oil and hot peppers in addition to pasta. The regional cuisine doesn't shy away from heavily spiced dishes; ginger and very hot peppers are among the favorites. Lampascioni are local wild onions known for their distinctive flavor. The region is also known for sausages; the *Lucanica* or *Lucanega* is an elaborate pork sausage and the *sopressato* sausage is oval, flat and flavored with ginger. The *Aglianico del Vulture* red wine is produced in the area around Rionero and known in other parts of Italy.

FESTIVAL FOCUS
La Sagra del Fagiolo
The Feast of the Bean
Sarconi

Each August in Sarconi you will find two days filled with food, folklore, and street artists. The beans of Sarconi are an *IGP* product. The acronym *IGP* means *Identificazione Geografica Protetta*; it is a designation given by the European Union when the quality and process of a product are dependent on the location of its production. There are bean products available for purchase at road-side stands, local restaurants highlight the beans on their menus, and educational programs are offered related to the importance of the beans in the area of Val d'Agri. The Val d'Agri is a lush area of Basilicata with mountains, lakes, and rivers. The town of Sarconi is located in the province of Potenza. You can obtain a map form the festival website showing the participating restaurants and stands throughout the town. Nearby places to visit include Moliterno Castle, Mount Sirino and Pietra del Pertusillo lake.

FESTIVALS OF BASILICATA

February
Festa del cioccolato
Chocolate Festival
Matera

May
Il Maggio di Accettura
Accettura May festival
Accettura

Sagra della Fragola
Strawberry Festival
Policoro

Sfilata (Cavalcata) dei Turchi
Procession of the Turks
Potenza

June
La Festa del Redentore
Feast of the Redeemer
Maratea

Festa del Raccolto
Harvest Festival
San Girogio Lucano

July
La Festa del Ritorno
The Feast of Return
Atella

Madonna della Bruna
Brown Madonna
Matera

August
La Sagra del Caciocavallo
The Feast of Caciocavallo Cheese
Rapone

La Sagra del Fagiolo
The Feast of the Bean
Sarconi

September
Salsiccia Festival
Sausage Festival
Cancellara

Sagra del Pecorino di Filiano
Filiano Pecorino Cheese Festival
Filiano

La Sagra della Varola
The Rite of Varola
Melfi

Sagra Dei Fichi Secchi
Dried Fig Festival
Miglionico

October
Giornate Medievale
Medieval Days
Brinidisi Montagna

Sagra della Castagna Munnaredda
Chestnut Festival
Munnaredda Tramutola

December
Sagra di San Martino
Feast of San Martino
Matera

Sagra delle Pettole
The Feast of Donuts
Montescaglioso

I love places that have an incredible history. I love the Italian way of life. I love the people. I love the attitude of Italians. — Elton John

7

CALABRIA

CALABRIA

Easily identified on a map as the "toe" of the Italian "boot," the Calabrian region is characterized by rugged terrain. Over 90% of the region is classified as hilly or mountainous and borders both the Tyrhennian and Ionian Seas. It is one of the oldest inhabited regions in Italy. Greek and Roman settlements of the area were later followed by centuries of foreign invaders including the French, Spanish and Austrians.

There is just under 500 miles of coastline in the region and many beaches on pristine waters. At its furthest point the Strait of Messina separates Calabria from Sicily. Just inland from the coast you are likely to find lots of vineyards and fruit orchards. Calabria has the second highest production of olive oil in the country and the second highest number of organic farmers, second only to Sicily. Calabria produces 80% of the worlds' bergamot citrus fruit. Bergamot is in the orange family, and although inedible, its essence is popular in fragrances and Earl Grey tea. Another popular citrus fruit grown here is the citron. Part of the lemon family, citron is larger than a lemon with a very bumpy texture; its rind is often boiled, then candied and included in fruitcake.

Swordfish and seafood are popular along the coast and the meat based dishes of the region use pork, lamb and goat as their sources for protein. Vegetables also figure prominently in the cuisine of the region with eggplants taking center stage. Nduja is a spicy and spreadable sausage made with the local pepperoncino (spicy peppers), great on bread or tossed with pasta. *Bucatini alla mollica* is prepared with sardines and fresh breadcrumbs. Look for the local *cipolla rossa di Tropea* (red onions) and for spicy sauces using pepperoncino and prepared *"alla carrettiera"* with ginger. Cow's milk cheeses are most popular, including *caciocavallo, mozarrella, scamorza,* and provolone.

FESTIVAL FOCUS
Sagra del Pesce Azzurro e della Cipolla Rossa
Feast of Blue Fish and Red Onions
Tropea

Every year on Largo Galluppi in the center of Tropea, July 27 marks the date of the Sagre del Pesce Azzurro e della Cipolla (the blue fish and red onion festival). The cipolla rossa di Tropea are red with a delicately sweet flavor and an important ingredient in local cuisine. During the celebration you can taste various traditional preparations of the local fish and special red onions from stands.

Tropea is in the province of Vibo Valentia and sits high on a cliff overlooking the town beach and the blue waters of the Gulf of Euphemia. It's a seaside resort town popular with tourists in summer. It has a very dramatic coastline referred to as the "coast of the Gods." Santa Maria della Isola is a monastery with stunning architecture and gardens on a small rocky island separate from the coastline. The popular *Gelateria Tonino* on Corso Vittorio Emanuele in the old town serves outlandish gelato flavors such as red onion, tuna, and spicy chili.

FESTIVALS OF CALABRIA

February
L'Abbaculo di Serra San Bruno
The Abbaculo of Serra San Bruno
Serra San Bruno

April
Festa della Pita
The Fir Tree Festival
Alessandria Del Carretto

Sagra della Primavera
Spring Festival
Castrovillari

July
Gran Galà del Pescespada
Grand Gala of the Swordfish
Bagnara Calabria

Sagra della cipolla rossa di Tropea e del Pesce
Azzurro Feast of the Red Onion and Blue Fish
Tropea

Sagra dei Fileia
Festival of Fileja Pasta
Vibo Valentia

August
Giornata del Contadino a Limbadi
Farmer Day in Limbadi
Limbadi

Festa di San Rocco
Feast of San Rocco
Palmi

Sagra dell' Antipasto Calabrese
Festival of Calabrian Appetizers
Sorianello

Pesce Spada
Swordfish Festival
Tonnara di Palmi

September
Pepperoncino Festival
Pepperoncino Festival
Diamante

Palio del Ciuccio
Palio of the Pacifier
Guardavalle

Sagra Dei Fichi Secchi
Dried Fig Festival
Luzzi

October
Sagra del Fungo Camigliatello Silano
The Festival of Camigliatello Silano Mushrooms
Camigliatello Silano

Festa del Fungho
Mushroom Festival
Mammola

Sagra della Castagna
Feast of the Chestnut
Serra Pedace

Capri on the Amalfi Coast in Italy is my ultimate holiday destination. – Vidal Sassoon

8

CAMPAGNA

CAMPANIA

Nothing conjures up the image of Italian sun, sand and La Dolce Vita like the Amalfi Coast in the region of Campania. The entire western edge borders the Tyrhennian Sea from just north of Naples south to the town of Sapri on the Gulf of Policastro. Even though Campania historically takes its name from the Latin "campus" (field) because of the plain around the area of Santa Maria Capua Vetere, it is mostly hilly and mountainous with very little plain. One of its largest mountains, Vesuvius, is famous for eruptions that left death and destruction in its wake, along with the archaeologically significant ruins at Pompeii and Herculaneum. It is the most industrialized area in southern Italy with the large ports of Naples and Salerno. Artisan and tourism industries are particularly important to the Amalfi Coast, Sorrento and the Islands of Capri and Ischia.

The cuisine of Campania is most closely related to what people in the rest of the world think of as Italian food: mozzarella, pizza, spaghetti with tomato sauce, espresso, pastries, Italian ice. For pizza purists, Naples is your mecca. Pizza is probably the best known product of Campania and the most popular styles are *alla napolitana* and *margherita*. Pizza originated as a flatbread and didn't evolve into the version known today until tomatoes were added sometime in the early 1800s. Be forewarned, once you have eaten a pizza here, it will be impossible not to compare it to any other in your future.

Coastal communities include seafood as the main staple of their diet while inland provinces such as Caserta and Avellino favor cheese and vegetables. Spaghetti, basked pastas, *baccala* (cod) and anything prepared *pizzaiola* (with tomatoes, oregano, garlic and white wine) all have a place at the Neopolitan dinner table. The most popular cheeses in the area are *Mozzarella di Bufala* (using buffalo milk), *fior di latte* mozzarella (made from cow's milk), ricotta (from sheep or buffalo milk), provolone (cow's milk) and *caciotta* (made from goat's milk). The lemons on the Amalfi coast produce their prized *limoncello* and the pastries of the region are some of the finest in Italy.

FESTIVAL FOCUS
Regata delle Antiche Repubbliche Marinare
Regatta of the Ancient Maritime Republics
Venice, Genoa, Pisa, Amalfi

The ancient maritime republic rivalries of Venice, Genoa, Pisa and Amalfi gather to compete in boating events. The event rotates each year between the four different locations. This is one of the finest and most popular folklore events in Italy. Huge boats constructed according to 12th century standards are propelled by eight rowers and one helmsman through a 1.25 mile long course along the coast. The hull of each vessel is painted according to the traditional colors of the respective city: red (Pisa), white (Genoa), green (Venice) and blue (Amalfi). Historical processions, dances and shows add to the event. Plan ahead for your travel arrangements.

FESTIVALS OF CAMPANIA

January
Festa di Sant'Antonio Abate
Festival of Saint Anthony the Abbot
Naples

March
Sagra del Maiale
The Pig Festival
Senerchia

April
Sagra del Carciofo
The Artichoke Festival
Capaccio Paestum

Sagra dei Prodotti Tipici
The Typical Products Festival
Cusano Mutri

May
Pizza Festival
The Pizza Festival
Naples

June
Regata Storica
Historical Regatta (month varies)
Amalfi

Sagra della Ciliega
The Cherry Festival
Forchia

Sagra degli Gnocchi
The Gnocchi Festival
Pantuliano

Sagra dell'Albicocca
The Apricot Festival
Sant'anastasia

July
Sagra dei Fusilli e del Pecorino
The Fusilli Pasta and Pecorino Cheese Festival
Ceppaloni

Festa del Mare
The Festival of the Sea
Conca dei Marini

Sagra del Limone
The Lemon Festival
Massa Lubrense

August
Historiae Volceiane
Historical Volcei
Buccino

Festa della Salsiccia Rossa a Castelpoto
Feast of the Red Sausage of Castelpoto
Castelpoto

Sagra della sfogliatella Santa Rosa
The Santa Rosa Sfogliatella Festival
Conca dei Marini

Sagra del Pomodorino
The Tomato Festival
Corbara

Festa del Limone
Lemon Festival
Massa Lubrense

Sagra del Pesce Azzurro
The Blue Fish Festival
Sapri

September
Sagra dell'Uva
Grape Festival
Capri

Sagra del Fico d'India
The Prickly Pear Festival
Castel Morrone

Sagra del Caciocavallo
The Caciocavallo Cheese Festival
Castelfranco In Miscano

Festa di San Gennaro
Feast of Saint Gerald
Naples

Festa della Pizza Mediterranea
Feast of Mediterranean Pizza
Naples

Sagra del Fusillo
The Fusilli Pasta Festival
Nocera Inferiore

Sagra del pesce
The Fish Festival
Positano

October
Sagra dell'olio d'oliva
Olive Oil Festival
Cervino

Sagra della castagna di Serino
The Festival of Serino Chestnuts
Serino

December
Festa del Torrone e del Croccantino
The Torrone and Croccantino Festival
San Marco dei Cavoti

NOTES

You may have the universe if I may have Italy.
— *Giuseppe Verdi*

9

EMILIA-ROMAGNA

EMILIA-ROMAGNA

Often overlooked on a first trip to Italy because of the more popular tourist destinations of Rome, Florence and Venice, if you consider yourself a lover of food or cars, a stop in this region is a must. Assembled from the two historic regions of Emilia and Romagna, both have their own languages: *Emilian* and *Romagnolo*, both considered romance languages, separate structurally from Italian and on the UNESCO Red Book of Endangered Languages list. The region is a center of excellence for some of the most famous names in the automobile world: Ferrari, Lamborghini, Maserati and Ducati.

Bologna, the regional capital, is home to the world's oldest university, The University of Bologna, founded in 1069. Bologna has several nicknames: "*la dotta*" (the learned) because of its atmosphere of higher learning; "*la grassa*" (the fat) because of the fabulous food; and "*la rossa*" (the red) because historically it was a center for communism and anti-fascist politics. Like San Gimignano in Tuscany, Bolognese families once built towers for their own protection and status. As many as 180 may have stood around the city at one time, but less than 20 can still be seen today. The most famous are two towers built by the Garisenda and Asinelli families that serve as landmarks of the historical center.

Zampone, stuffed pigs feet, are a specialty of the area. But if stuffed pigs feet aren't your thing, you are in luck, there is plethora of other specialties to choose from. Stuffed pastas and their choice of fillings vary throughout the region. *Tortellini in brodo* and *tagliatelle Bolognese* should be on everyone's menu wish list. Pork products are a highlight of the region's cuisine for meat-eaters and stuffed vegetables are a popular side dish. The region is home to favorites such as mortadella, various salamis, *pancetta, coppa, prosciutto di Parma* and the prized *culatello*. Since the eastern border of the region is on the Adriatic Sea, there is a great base of seafood in that area. Cervia, a town along the Adriatic coastline, is famous for its salt production and has festivals to celebrate their product achievements each year. The famous Aceto Balsamico has a stringent production process and quite frankly, you haven't tasted balsamic vinegar until you have had some of this blissful nectar produced in Modena and Reggio Emilia. Parma's parmesan cheese is the most famous cheese of the region, and perhaps the world, but other fine cheeses of *parmigiana reggiano* and *grana padano* are also produced here.

FESTIVAL FOCUS
La Festa della Polenta
The Feast of Polenta
Tossignano

The polenta festival in Tossignano has been in continuous operation since 1622, except for the years during World War II. The festival is held on the last day of Carnival each year, rain or shine. Traditionally, polenta cooked with sausage and cheese is served to villagers starting at noon and to visitors after three o'clock. This village is about 19 miles southeast of Bologna and has less than 400 full-time inhabitants. During lean times, polenta was the bread of the poor. With the discovery of corn in America, the making of polenta made from corn meal spread wherever the corn was grown starting in the 1700s.

FESTIVALS OF EMILIA ROMAGNA

January
Biso Notte
Biso Night
Faenza

Festa di Sant'Ilario
Feast of St. Hilary
Parma

February
Carnevale di Cento
Carnival of Cento
Cento

La Festa della Polenta
The Feast of Polenta
Tossignano

Sagra dei Maccheroni
Macaroni Festival
Ponticelli di Imola

March
Sagra dei Salumi e del Tartufo
Feast of Italian Meats and Truffles
Brisighella

April
Sagra della Pié Fritta
Festival of Fried Pie' (dough)
Fontanelice

May
Sagra dell'Asparago Verde di Altedo
Green Asparagus Festival
Altedo di Malalbergo

Sposalizio del Mare
Sea Wedding
Cervia

Festa delle Arzdore
Feast of Arzdore
Dozza

Palio di Ferrara
Ancient Horse Race of Ferrara
Ferrara

Sagra della Fragola
Strawberry Festival
Lagosanto

Maschere Italiane a Parma
Italian Masks in Parma
Parma

Sagra della Seppia e Dalla Canocchia
Cuttlefish and Mantis Shrimp Fair
Porto Garibaldi

Festa del Cappelletto
Festival of Cappelletto
Ravenna

Antica Sagra della Porchetta
Roast Suckling Pig Festival
Saludecio

June
Feste Medioevali
Medieval Feasts
Brisighella

Sagra dell'Albicocco
Apricot Festival
Casalfiumanese

July
Sagra del Tortellino Tipico di Reno Centese
Reno Centese Tortellini Festival
Reno Centese

Sagra del Cocomero
Watermelon Festival
Imola

August
Grande Rustida dei Pescatori
Fish tasting cooked by the fishermen of Cesenatico
Casenatico

Tradizionale Fiera del Parmigiano-Reggiano
Traditional Parmesan Cheese Festival
Casina

Fiera dell'Aglio di Voghiera
Garlic Festival
Castello di Belriguardo

September
Antica Sagra del Monticino
Ancient Festival Monticino
Brisighella

Festa del Garganello
The Garganello Festival
Codrignano di Imola

Rievocazione Storica del Barbarossa
Reenactment of Barbarossa
Medicina

Festival del Prosciutto di Parma
Prosciutto Festival
Parma

Perdono di Canossa
Pardon of Canossa
Reggio nell'Emilia

Sorbara Wine Festival
Sorbara Wine Festival
Sorbara

October
Fiera Nazionale del Tartufo Nero di Fragno
National Fair of the Fragno Black Truffle
Calestano

Sagra della Salamina da Sugo al Cucchiaio
Sausage Festival
Madonna Boschi

Festa Della Castagna Di Marola
Chestnut Festival of Marola
Marola

Fiera della Zucca
Pumpkin Festival
Reggiolo

November
Sagra della Pera Volpina
Volpina Pear Festival
Brisighella

Sagra del Tartufo
Truffle Festival
Brisighella

Festa dei Vignaioli
Winegrowers Festival
Predappio Alta

Sagra del Tartufo
Truffle Festival
Savigno

Sagra del Formaggio di Fossa
Fossa Cheese Festival
Talamello

December
Sagra dell'Olio Extra Vergine
Extra Virgin Oil Festival
Brisighella

Sagra del Formaggio di Fossa
Fossa Cheese Festival
Sogliano Sul Rubicone

NOTES

Open my heart and you will see graved inside of it, "Italy".
  – Robert Browning

10

FRIULI-VENEZIA GIULIA

FRIULI-VENEZIA GIULIA

Despite the name of this region, the city of Venice (Venezia) is NOT a part of it, albeit close by. Like the Trentino-Alto Adige region, Friuli-Venezia Giulia was historically two different regions. It borders Austria to the north and Slovenia to the east. It sits on the Adriatic Sea to the south and transitions to an alpine climate in its north. Friuli was part of the Venetian territory in the 1400s and the Trieste and Gorizia provinces were part of the Austro-Hungarian empire. At one point every invader seems to have passed through here whether it be Atilla the Hun or Nazis. While standard Italian is the predominant language, there are three dialects also spoken here: *Furlan, Venetian, and Triestine.*

Like the other northernmost regions of Italy, neighbors and border changes have had significant influences in some of the traditional dishes in the area. Whether you are in search of the very Italian prosciutto of San Daniele, Friuli sauerkraut made with turnips, *Friulian* strudel made with ricotta cheese, or top-notch wines, you'll encounter great food and great people. Unless you are a professional foodie you might not be able to taste the difference between San Daniele prosciutto and that of its rival prosciutto di Parma; a tip to tell the difference: the San Danielle retains the foot of the pig.

The wines may represent a small portion of Italy's overall production but they are highly regarded. There are seven DOC zones in Friuli, but if you only have time to travel a few of the rustic wine roads focus on the *Isonzo, Colli* and *Colli Orientali.* If wines aren't your thing, coffee and grappa also have some fine producers here.

Cividale del Friuli and Aquilea are two important historical centers. Aquilea was founded in 181 BC, was an important city in the Roman Empire and roman ruins are still around for touring. Cividale's ancient market was on the trade route between the Adriatic Sea and the Alps to the

North. The Forum Juli (Julius's Market) was founded here and the name eventually morphed into Friuli.

FESTIVAL FOCUS
Palio di San Donato
Race of San Donato
Cividale

For one weekend each August, Cividale, its five neighborhoods and 500 participants are transported back to medieval times. Founded by none other than Julius Caesar, the start of Cividale's Palio can be traced back to August in the year 1368 when a city decree declared the Palio di San Donato should be repeated in perpetuity. That lasted until 1797 when it was cancelled (thank you, Napoleon), but then reinstituted in 2000.

Starting at seven o'clock Friday night and continuing through Sunday, entertainment, jugglers, parades and drumbeats can be heard in Piazza Duomo and each of the town neighborhoods. Saturday continues with the archery, cross-bow and foot race competitions. There are reconstructed medieval street markets and taverns throughout the town. All of the festivities culminate on Sunday when the most victorious of the five neighborhoods is declared the winner.

FESTIVALS OF FRIULI-VENEZIA GIULIA

January
Sagra Salsicce e Polenta
Feast of Sausage and Polenta
Ferentillo

February
Mascherata a Remanzacco
Mascherade of Remanzacco
Remanzacco

Palio di San Giusto
Palio di San Giusto
Trieste

March
La Sagra delle Rane
Feast of Frogs
Travesio

April
Festa delle Cape
Seafood Festival
Lignano Pineta

May
Festa dell'Asparago di Bosco, del Radicchio di Montagna e dei Funghi di Primavera
Mushrooms, Woodland Asparagus and Mountain Radicchio Festival
Arta Terme

June
Festa del Formaggio
Cheese Festival
Fagnigola

Festa del Prosciutto di San Daniele
Festival of San Daniele Prosciutto
San Daniele del Friuli

July
Perdòn de Barbana
Perdòn de Barbana
Grado

Sagra dei Gamberi
Shrimp Festival
Zoppola

August
Sagra del Panzerotto
Panzerotto Festival (similar to a calzone)
Cavazzo Carnico

Palio di San Donato
Race of San Donato
Cividale

Sagra Delle Patate Godia
Godia Potato Festival
Godia

September
Festa dei Funghi dell'Ambiente
Mushroom Festival in the Environment
Budoia

Rievocazione Storica Rinascimentale con Mercato
Historical Renaissance Re-enactment with Market
Cormons

October
Mosta Regionale della Mela
Regional Exhibition of Apples
Mereto di Tomba

Festa della Zucca
Pumpkin Festival
Venzone

December
Sapori di Carnia
Flavors of Meat Festival
Raveo

Methinks I will not die quite happy without having seen
something of that Rome – Sir Walter Scott

11

LAZIO

LAZIO

Lazio is home to the famous and ancient cities of Rome and Vatican City. But there is more to the Lazio region than simply visiting Italy's largest city and the most heavily touristic points of interest. The beautiful medieval city of Vitterbo, Lago di Bolsena for relaxation and recreation, and the Etruscan ruins in Tarquinia are all worth the effort and a little more off the beaten path. It borders the Tyrhennian Sea and hosts a string of beach resorts; many in driving distance from Rome. The name Lazio is derived from the Latin word *latium*, after the ancient tribe of Latins in the pre-Roman era; it became part of unified Italy in 1870.

Volcanic activity in the area fertilized the soil to support the growth of olive trees, vines, fruits and nuts. Pasta is a main part of any meal along with seafood from the coast, pork, lamb and veal. *Carciofi alla giudia* were introduced by the Jewish community, and are deep fried in olive oil and served as an appetizer at many restaurants. Traditional pasta sauces include carbonara (egg, cheese and *guanciale* which is pork cheek similar to bacon), *amatriciana* (guanciale, pecorino cheese and tomatoes) and the very simple yet tasty *cacio e pepe* (pecorino romano cheese and pepper). Veal saltimbocca, meaning literally "jump in mouth" and *spaghetti alle vongole* (with clams) are also popular dishes.

FESTIVAL FOCUS
Sagra del Carciofo Romanesco
Feast of the Roman Artichoke
Ladispoli

The Sagra del Carciofo Romanesco in Ladispoli outside of Rome claims to be the first festival in the world honoring the artichoke. Ladispoli is just over twenty miles west of Rome on the Mediterranean coastline. Started in 1950 to promote artichokes and especially tourism in Ladispoli, the festival has endured and is held in early April each year over a three-day period. Leading up to the event, the restaurants in the area have highlighted the use of artichokes and offer fixed price menus. There are stands for tasting the artichokes as well as musical entertainment and cooking demonstrations.

FESTIVALS OF LAZIO

January
Sagra della Bruschetta
Bruschetta Festival
Casaprota

Sagra delle Frittelle
Festival of Cauliflower Pancakes
Tuscania

February
Carnevale Storico
Historical Carnival
Ronciglione

Pizza Festival
The Pizza Festival
Montoro Superiore

Sagra della Polenta
Polenta Festival
Sermoneta

March
Festa di San Giuseppe
Feast of St. Joseph
Rome

April
Sagra del Biscotto
Festival of Biscuit
Bomarzo

Sagra degli Gnocchi
Gnocchi Festival
Riofreddo

Sagra dell'Asparago Selvatico
Wild Asparagus Festival
Torrita Tiburina

Sagra del Carciofo Romanesco
Feast of the Roman Artichoke
Ladispoli

May
Festa Madonna del Monte - Storia Barabbata
Madonna del Monte Festival - History
Barabbata Marta ›

June
Infiorata di Genzano
Flower Festival in Genzano
Genzano

La Sagra delle Fragole
The Strawberry Festival
Nemi

Festa di San Giovanni Laterano
Feast of St. John Lateran
Rome

July
Sagra Delle Pesche
Peach Festival
Castel Gandolfo

La Festa de Noiantri
The Festa de Noiantri
Rome

August
Sagra degli Spaghetti all'Amatriciana
Spaghetti Amatriciana Festival
Amatrice

September
Sagra della Porchetta di Ariccia
Feast of Porchetta of Ariccia
Ariccia

October
Sagra dell'uva
Grape Festival
Marino

Festa della Castagna
Chestnut Festival
San Martino di Ciminio

Sagra dell'Uva
Grape Festival
Zagarolo

Thou paradise of exiles, Italy! – Percy Bysshe Shelley

12

LIGURIA

LIGURIA

Liguria is a narrow region that follows the coastline of the blue Mediterranean Sea from the border of France south to Tuscany, and includes the Maritime Alps and the Ligurian Alps. The only flat parts of the region are where the land touches the sea. Home to the "Italian Riviera," Liguria has sandy beaches, port cities, fishing villages, mountain villages, and dramatic shoreline cliffs. One of the ancient maritime areas of Italy, the Ligurians are known as great seafarers. Several events take place along the coast between June and September that involve boat regattas. Liguria is home to the famed Cinque Terre (5 villages), a major tourist draw along the southern Ligurian coast, just north of the Tuscan border. The five pastel, jewel box-like villages cling to the small ports and cliffs along the coastline. You can hike and walk between villages facing various levels of difficulty.

Seafood, basil pesto, lemons, *farinata* and focaccia are the five foods that spring to mind when Liguria is included in travel plans. There are festivals dedicated to each of these items between April and May. Pesto is made from a blend of fresh local basil, parmesan, pecorino, olive oil, pine nuts and garlic and is commonly used on pasta and in soup. Seafood is a main staple, and Ligurian tables also include herbs from the mountain hillsides, fruits and vegetables.

A visit to Liguria isn't complete without stopping by one of the *friggitorie* fry shops or stands. A Ligurian version of "fast food," the fry shops serve up tender fried seafood in a cone or on a stick and are quite tasty. Between the friggitorie and bake shops serving freshly made focaccia with cheese, eating on the fly is easy throughout Liguria. Complete the meal with a glass of sweet, white Cinque Terre produced dessert wine called *"Sciacchetra"* (pronounced shock-e-trah) for a true taste of the region.

FESTIVAL FOCUS
Sagre del Pesce
Feast of the Fish
Camogli

Since 1952, on the second Sunday of May a gigantic frying pan is set up in Camogli's Piazza Columbo to fry fish and feed the community. How do you feed an entire village with fish? You need a lot of fisherman and a gigantic frying pan! The current pan is 13 feet in diameter and weighs approximately 4 tons. Frying pans of the past are displayed on a wall along the Largo Simonetti in town. The fishermen set out to sea against a backdrop of bonfires and fish all night before returning to the village with their catch.

This public fish fry celebrates the patron saint of fisherman, San Fortunato. Legend has it that in 1710 some *Camoglini* sailed to Civitavecchia en route to Rome to ask the Pope to name a patron saint for their fishermen. San Fortunato was the lucky saint chosen and a statue was brought back on the ship to Camogli. On the return journey, they were surprised by a storm, prayed to their Saint Fortunato, the storm subsided and everyone returned safely to Camogli. An urn with the relics of San Fortunato is located in the Basilica Santa Maria Assunta in Camogli.

FESTIVALS OF LIGURIA

February
Sagra della Mimosa
Mimosa Festival
Pieve Ligure

Festa di Primavera
Spring Festival
Santa Margherita

Festa di San Benedetto
Feast of St. Benedict
Taggia

March
Rassegna dell'Olio d'Oliva
Exhibition of Olive Oil
Balestrino

Festa di San Giuseppe
Feast of St. Joseph
La Spezia

April
Festa delle Biscette a Solva
Festival of the Biscette in Solva
Solva

May
Sagra del Pesce
Feast of the Fish
Camogli

Festa della Focaccia con il Formaggio
Festival of Focaccia Bread with Cheese
Recco

June
Palio Marinaro del Tigullio
Sea Faring Festival of Tigullio
Chiavari, Rapallo, Lavagna

Festa e Palio di San Pietro
Party and Palio di San Pietro
Genoa

Regata delle Antiche Repubbliche Marinare
The Regatta of the Ancient Maritime Republics
Genoa

July
Sagra del Muscolo
Mussels Festival
Cadimare

Festa al Paraiso
Feast of Paradise
Imperia

Festa del Mare
Festival of the Sea
Levanto

Sagra delle Rose and Sagra delle Pesche
Feast of the Rose and Peach
Pogli d'Ortovero

August
Stella Maris
Stella Maris
Camogli

Festa del Mare
Festival of the Sea
Diano Marina

Festa del Mare & Palio del Golfo
Festival of the Sea & Palio of the Gulf
La Spezia

Torta dei Fieschi
Historical Wedding Celebration "Fieschi's Cake"
Lavagna

September
Commemorazione della Battaglia Napoleonica
Commemoration of the Napoleonic Battle
Loano

Sagra della Lumache
Feast of Snails
Molini di Triora

Sagra dell'Acciuga Fritta
Fried Anchovy Festival
Monterosso al Mare

Regata Storica dei Rioni
Historical Regatta of the Districts
Noli

Sagra del Pigato
Pigato Wine Festival
Salea di Albegna

Sagra dell'Uva
Grape Festival
Varazze

Sagra dell'Uva
Grape Festival
Vezzano Ligure

October
Sagra della Farinata
Feast of Chickpea Fritters
Voltri

November
Olioliva
Olive Oil Festival
Imperia

December
Confuoco
Festival with Fire
Pietra Ligure & Savona

Traveling is the ruin of all happiness! There's no looking at a building after seeing Italy – Fanny Burney

13

LOMBARDIA

LOMBARDY

Named after the *Longobards* or long beards (a Germanic tribe that ruled the area beginning in the 6th century), Lombardy is home to the fashionista city of Milan and the famous lakes of Como, Maggiore, Iseo and Garda. The region is approximately half fertile plains and half mountains, bordered by Switzerland on the north. The many rivers and lakes in this region contribute to its agricultural riches. There are 12 provinces, eight UNESCO world heritage sites, the famous La Scala opera house, and one of the world's most famous paintings, "The Last Supper," housed in the refectory of Basilica di Santa Maria delle Grazie.

An area very rich in agriculture, you are more likely to find the short-grained rice of the area used in risotto rather than pasta on the dish at home. In the Brescia, Bergamo and Valtellina areas polenta is quite common. Lombardy is home to dishes prepared *"alla Milanese"* style, particularly veal cutlets dipped in egg and bread crumbs then fried until golden brown, as well as *osso bucco*, boiled meats and vegetable soups. Popular cheeses produced in the region include *robiola, crescenza, taleggio*, gorgonzola, and *grana padano*.

FESTIVAL FOCUS
Festa del Risotto
Feast of Risotto
Villimpenta

The town of Villimpenta is 115 miles east of Milan, nestled on the border of Lombardia and the Veneto. The town is dominated by the 114 foot high walls of Castello di Villimpenta which dates back to the 11th century when it was constructed as a fortified monastery. The Festa del Risotto in Villimpenta is held after the rice paddies have been planted and extends over several weekends in June each year.

Riso alla Pilota is served from a large tent set up with volunteers managing gigantic vats of rice and distributing the dishes to the thousands of attendees. It is named for the *pilotato*, huskers who hulled the rice. The rice is cooked then mixed with pork, pancetta, garlic and cheese. There is a musical attraction on the stage each night accompanied by dancing. The proceeds from this festa fund several community activities throughout the year.

FESTIVALS OF LOMBARDY

January
Festa Sant'Antonio Abate
Feast of Saint Anthony the Abbot
Volongo

February
Carnevale di Bagolino
Carnival of Bagolino
Bagolino

March
Palio dei Falo
Bonfire Palio
Lezzeno

Sagra del Polentone
Feast of Polenta
Retorbido

April
Sagra del Gnocchi
Feast of Gnocchi
Albavilla

May
Festa degli Asparagi e delle Fragole
Feast of Asparagus and Strawberries
Isola della Scala

Sagra dell Asparago
Feast of Asparagus
San Benedetto Po

June
Festa del Pescatore
The Fisherman's Feast
Lainate

Sagra del Melone
Feast of Melon
Viadana

Festa del Risotto
Feast of Risotto
Villimpenta

July
Festa dei Pizzoccheri
Feast of Pizzoccheri
Teglia

August
La Sagra degli Gnocchi e delle Salamelle
The Festival of Gnocchi and Sausage
Pognana Lario

September
Sagra del Nazionale Gorgonzola
National Festival of Gorgonzola
Gorgonzola

La Sagra del Salame dell'Oca
Festival of Goose Salami
Mortara

October
La Sagra dell'Offella
The Feast of the Offelle (biscuits)
Parona

Sagra dal Nedar
Duck Festival
San Benedetto Po

Festa Della Polenta
Festival of Polenta
Vigasio

NOTES

Everything you see I owe to pasta. – *Sofia Loren*

14

LE MARCHE

THE MARCHES

This region of Italy is very hilly and draws travelers in with its rich heritage and seaside resort towns. It sits in the middle of the Italian Adriatic coastline and is surrounded by the better known provinces of Tuscany and Umbria to the west, Lazio and Abruzzo to the south, and Emilia Romagna and the Republic of San Marino to the north.

Regional meat delicacies including salt and air-cured pork are just the tip of the iceberg. *Coppa* and *porchetta* (herb roasted pork on a spit) are also popular throughout the region. Like other areas of Italy, cheese and olives are mainstays of the local agricultural production. *Marchigiani* love their grilled meats which make up a large portion of their diet. In addition to beef, other popular meats include chicken, rabbit, game birds, and goose. The region is home to the *Formaggio di Fossa* and *Casciotta di Urbino* cheeses. The Formaggio di Fossa is cured in limestone holes in the ground and has a strong flavor. Olive trees are used for olive oil production and for olive dishes. A well-known specialty from the Ascoli Piceno province is the *"olive all'ascolana."* The fleshy green olives are stuffed with meat, breaded and the deep fried.

Vincisgrassi is a signature baked pasta dish of the region. It is a béchamel sauce-based lasagna that includes meat and has 'a longer preparation time. Modern versions of this recipe call for tomatoes to be included but more ancient recipes call for prosciutto and truffles instead. Campofilone pasta is known for using free range chicken eggs and non-gmo durum wheat, which results in a delicate pasta that is high in protein. There are sixteen black and white truffle varieties found here, with the truffle centers being Sant'Angelo in Vado and Acqualegna in northern Marche. *Stoccafisso* (dried cod) and *brodetto* fish stew are popular seafood dishes. The region's spirits production includes Mistra, Anisetta, red and white wines.

FESTIVAL FOCUS
La Sagra dei Maccheroncini
The Feast of Macaroni
Campofilone

Between Ascoli Piceno and Ancona and only a seven minute drive from the Adriatic coast, the town of Campofilone has hosted the *Sagra dei Maccheroncini* for over 50 years. This ode to that delicately elegant pasta we know as angel hair, is served with traditional meat sauce to attendees at long tables laid out at four points throughout the town. Spoken about in texts since 1400, there is no water added to the flour and eggs and it is cut so thin it only takes a minute in boiling water to cook. The "Maccheroncini di Campofilone" received I.G.P. recognition in 2013. I.G.P. means Indicazione Geografica Protetta (Protected Geographical Indication). The party continues at Piazza San Bartolomeo for four nights in early August with a different musical act providing the entertainment each evening.

FESTIVALS OF THE MARCHE

February
Carnevale Storico del Piceno
Historical Carnival of Piceno
Ascoli Piceno, Castignano, Offida and Pozza

Carnevale di Fano
Carnival of Fano
Fano

Corrida del bo finto
The Fake Bullfight
Offida

April
Fritto Misto all'Italiana
Italian Style Mixed Fried Food Festival
Ascoli Piceno

May
Fiera di San Ciriaco
Fair of Saint Ciriaco
Ancona

Sagre del Carciofo
Artichoke Festival
Montelupone

June
Veregra Street Festival
Veregra Street Festival
Montegranaro

August
Giostra della Quintana
Giostra della Quintana
Ascoli Piceno

La Sagra dei Maccheroncini
Macaroni Festival
Campofilone

Sagra Coniglio in Porchetta
Feast of Rabbit in Porchetta
Serra San Quirico

Festa del Duca
Festival of the Duke
Urbino

September
Festival Internazionale del Brodetto e delle Zuppe di Pesce
International Festival of Brodetto and Fish Soup
Fano

Pane Nostrum
Our Bread
Senigallia

October
Fiera Nazionale del Tartufo Bianco
National Fair of White Truffles
Acqualagna

Sagra dell'Uva
Grape Festival
Cupramontana

Fiera Nazionale del Tartufo Bianco di Pergola
National Fair of White Truffle from Pergola
Pergola

Festival Nazionale delle Marche Tartufo Bianco
National Festival of Marche White Truffle
Sant'Angelo in Vado

I love the simplicity, the ingredients, the culture, the history and the seasonality of Italian cuisine. In Italy people do not travel. They cook the way grandma did, using fresh ingredients and what is available in season. — Anne Burrell

15

MOLISE

MOLISE

Molise shares the name of a castle and ancient warlord family. It is one of the least touristy parts of Italy, is mountainous and claims a small amount of Adriatic coastline. This is not a part of Italy filled with five star hotels, but one filled with impressive ruins and historic attractions that are off the beaten track. The cuisine of Molise is similar to Abruzzo and in fact, it used to be part of Abruzzo until the 1960s. Because of its varied landscape and historical ruins, Molise can satisfy every type of sports and history enthusiast.

Bruschetta and meat dishes are popular antipasti, and the variety of meats includes *Capocolli, Salsiccie al finocchio, soppressata, ventricina, frascateglie*, and *sanguinaccio*. Different types of pasta are served for the first course; common types are *cavatelli*, traditional lasagna, or *maccheroni* served with a lamb or goat ragu. A specialty of the Campobasso province is *calcioni di ricotta*. These calcioni are essentially fried mini-calzones or ricotta fritters stuffed with *scamorza* (similar to mozzarella) parsley and prosciutto. Organ meats (such as tripe), lamb, rabbit, and pork are popular second courses here. *Caciocavallo* is a popular cow's milk cheese and a Termoli mainstay is its *zuppa di pesce* (seafood soup) along the limited amount of coastline in the region.

FESTIVAL FOCUS
La 'Ndocciata
La 'Ndocciata
Agnone

An ancient festival of light with Pagan beginnings, 'Ndocciata is now a Christian feast of Christmas light in Agnone. *'Ndocce* are torches made from white fir tree, straw and string. When lit, the resin from the tree creates a crackling sound; a great crackling sound, makes a "good" 'ndocce. Starting at 5:30 p.m. on Christmas Eve, after the bell tower in the church of St. Anthony rings, the participants light their torches and walk through the town. The procession begins at the edge of town, near the hospital, and continues toward the church of St. Anthony. At the same time others from the different districts and quarters also proceed through town creating a "streets of fire" effect. Animals, wagons and shepherds are included in the parade, ending in Piazza Plebiscito where the torches are added to a great bonfire called "brotherhood" to burn away negative effects of the past year and look toward the new one.

FESTIVALS OF MOLISE

January
Festa de Sant'Antonio Abate
Festival of Saint Anthony the Abbot
Larino

May
La Sfilata dei carri di Larino
The Parade of Larino Carriages
Larino

June
La Fiera delle Cipolle
The Fair of Onions
Isernia

July
Festa della Mietitura
Feast of the Harvest
Castellino del Biferno

La Festa del Grano
The Festival of Wheat
Jelsi

Festa di Sant'Anna - Sfilata dei Covoni
Feast of Saint Anna - Parade of Sheaves
Pescolanciano

August
Festa del Ritorno dell'Emigrante
Festival of the Return of Emigrants
Campolieto

La Pezzata Capracotta
The Pieces of Capracotta
Capracotta

Sagra di Peperuol e Baccala
Festival of Peperuol and Codfish
Frosolone

Sagra della Ciff e Ciaff
Festival of Ciff and Ciaff
Pescopennatro

Regata e Processione di S. Basso a Termoli
Regatta and Procession of Saint Basso in Termoli
Termoli

September
La Sagra dell'Uva di Riccia
The Grape Festival of Riccia
Riccia

October
Sagra dell'Uva
Grape Festival
Poggio Sannita

December
La 'Ndocciata di Agnone
The N'Docciata di Agnone
Agnone

La Faglia di Oratino
The Fault of Oratino
Oratino

NOTES

Italy is a dream that keeps on returning for the rest of your life.
— Anna Akhmatova

16

PIEMONTE

PIEDMONT

Settled by Celts and conquered by Romans, the Piemonte has a strong agricultural economy and is also home to giants of industry such as Fiat automobiles and Lavazza coffee. It is surrounded on three sides by the Alps and shares borders with France, Switzerland and four other Italian provinces. It is one of the largest land provinces in Italy, second only to Sicily. Though it is mostly mountainous, it has large areas of hills and plains.

Once a hidden gem, Piemonte tourism has increased steadily in recent years. The prestigious wines *Barolo*, *Barbaresco*, *Asti Spumante* and *Moscato d'Asti* all call the Piemonte home. The farming, peasant traditions, and geographic position influence the food. In fact, the slow food movement started in the town of Bra in 1986. In the northwest mountainous region, foods based in peasant traditions are predominant; in the lowland areas and cities, French influence can be felt in the cuisine.

The Piemonte is perhaps best known for its wine and white truffles. In addition to the many festivals celebrating wine and truffles of the region, cheese, beans, risotto, and polenta are also focus foods for feasts. Plan to visit Alba for truffles and truffle-infused products. Head to the Langhe area for wine tasting. For top-notch risotto travel to Vercelli and its rice paddies. If you visit Torino, enjoy great coffee and chocolate at the cafes.

FESTIVAL FOCUS
Storico Carnevale di Ivrea
Historical Carnival of Ivrea
Ivrea

It's a great Italian food fight! Oranges are the ammunition of this battle royale in the northern Italian town of Ivrea. Referred to as the "largest food fight" in Italy, the Battle of the Oranges engages over 5,000 participants inflicting pain by hurling 60 tons of blood oranges at each other. Ivrea, north of Turin and west of Milan, imports an entire train full of oranges from Sicily each year for the event.

The battle is based on stories of real people from the rebellion 900 years ago. At this period in time, the *jus primae noctae* or "right of the first night" allowed the local lord to sleep with a bride the night before her wedding. As the story goes, the *mugnaia* (miller's daughter), went to the castle the night before her wedding, wielded a knife, murdered the lord and cut his head off. The locals then started a three day rebellion which is represented by the throwing of the oranges.

Activities include historical parades, feasts, and of course the famous orange fight. *Aranceri* (orange handlers) on fifty carts battle the aranceri from the nine pedestrian teams. Spectators are strongly advised to purchase and wear at all times the *beretto frigio*; this red stocking cap identifies the innocent onlookers hoping to escape errant oranges. Nets are strung throughout the parade route with designated areas for spectators to gather beneath for protection. The timing of this festival coincides with traditional carnival period each year, driven by the number of weeks before the Christian holiday of Easter.

FESTIVALS OF THE PIEDMONT

January
Fagiolata
Fagiolata Soup Festival
Badia di Dulzago

Sagra del Salam 'd Patata
Festival of Potatoes and Sausage
Settimo Rottaro

February
Storico Carnevale di Ivrea
Historical Carnival of Ivrea
Ivrea

May
Corsa dei Buoi
Race of the Oxen
Asigliano Vercellese

Sagra del Risotto
Risotto Festival
Sessame

Sagra Dell Aspargo
Asparagus Festival
Valmacca

June
Festa della Fragola
Strawberry Festival
Borgo San Martino

Festa dell'Aglio Nuovo
Festival of New Garlic
Caraglio

July
Sagra della Focaccia al Formaggio e delle Trofie al Pesto
Festival of Cheese Focaccia and Trofie Pasta with Pesto
Casalgermelli

Sagra del Peperone Quadrato d'Asti
Festival of Square Peppers of Asti
Costigliole d'Asti

August
Mangialonga La Morra
Mangialonga of La Morra
La Morra

Sagra della Pesca Ripiena
Festival of Stuffed Fish
Rocca Canavese

September
Investitura del Podestà
Investiture of the Mayor
Alba

Festa delle Sagre Astigiane
Asti's Festival of Festivals
Asti

Cheese!
Cheese! Festival in Bra
Bra

October
Fiera Internazionale del Tartufo Bianco d'Alba
International Fair of the Alba White truffle
Alba

Il Baccanale del Tartufo
The Truffle Bacchanal
Alba

Il Borgo si Rievoca
Evoking the Historic Borgo
Alba

Palio degli Asini
Race of the Donkeys
Alba

November

Fiera Nazionale del Tartufo

National Truffle Fair

San Sebastiano Curone

December

Fiera del Bue Grasso

Fat Ox Fair

Carrù

NOTES

Life is a combination of magic and pasta. – Federico Fellini

17

SARDEGNA

SARDINIA

Sardinia is the second largest island in the Mediterranean Sea (Sicily is the largest) and has been settled since pre-historic times. At different times the island has been held by the Spanish (twice) and the Austrians. Each of the eight provinces has its own indigenous Sardinian language that enjoys "equal dignity" with Italian as declared by regional law. The Strait of Bonifacio separates French neighbor Corsica to the north. With an unspoiled terrain, fabulous beaches, and resorts, tourism continues to grow on the island. Except for some of the ancient port cities, most settlement was inland to avoid the marshy coastlines, but in the last 70 years they started to be developed.

There are over 7,000 prehistoric *nuraghe* found around the island. Nuraghe are cylindrical stone structures made of basalt and are stacked without using any bonding agents to keep them in place. Along with its 1,125 miles of coastline, Sardinia also has mountains that receive enough snow in winter to support some alpine ski areas. Passenger ferries arrive at Sardinia from the ports of Genoa, Livorno, Civitavecchia, Naples, Palermo, and Trapani in Italy, as well as from Nice, France and Tunis, Tunisia.

Shepherd and fisherman are two of the most popular occupations on this island where the sheep are said to outnumber the residents. Three of its sheep's milk cheeses have earned a quality DOP label: the *pecorino romano*, *pecorino sardo* and *fiore sardo*. Quite unusual, the *casu marzu* is a Sardinian cheese known to contain live insect larvae. Caviar made from mullet eggs known as *bottarga* is popular around Oristano. Suckling pig and wild boar roasted or cooked in stews with beans and vegetables are also popular.

FESTIVAL FOCUS
Festa dei Candelieri
Feast of Candlesticks
Sassari

The Festa dei Candelieri was imported to Sardinia by settlers from Pisa. It is over 500 years old and takes place each year on August 14. Music and drums can be heard in the streets in the days leading up to the festival. There are giant candles weighing over 800 pounds each from the ten trade guilds, which are offered to the Madonna in memory of her ending the plague in the city in 1652.

The festivities begin in the morning at 10 a.m. when the candles at each guild location are decorated with ribbons to prepare for their journey through town. There are different ceremonies during the day leading up to the parade of the candles through town. The parade ceremony starts at 5 p.m. and the candles begin to dance through the town at 6 p.m.. Guild members transport them through the streets beginning at Piazza Castello and ending at the Church of Santa Maria di Betlem.

FESTIVALS OF SARDINIA

January
Fuoco di Sant'Antonio Abate a Dorgali
Fire of Sant'Antonio Abate in Dorgali
Dorgali

Sagra del Maiale Montresino
Pig Festival Montresino
Montresta

February
Festa di Mamuthones (Carnevale)
Feast of the Mamuthones (Carnival)
Mamoiada

Sa Sartiglia di Oristano
The Sartiglia of Oristano
Oristano

May
Festa di Sant'Efisio
Feast of Saint Efisio in Cagliari
Cagliari

Girotonno
Tuna Festival
Carloforte

Cavalcata Sarda a Sassari
Sardinian Ride in Sassari
Sassari

June
Sagre del Pesce
Fish Festival
Olbia Tempio

Sa Batalla de Seddori in Sanluri
Battle of Sanluri
Sanluri

July
Sagra Estiva in Onore di Nostra Signora di Bonaria a Cagliari
Summer Festival in Honor of Our Lady of Bonaria in Cagliari
Cagliari

Ardia di San Costantino a Pozzomaggiore
Ardia of San Costantino in Pozzomaggiore
Pozzomaggiore

S'Ardia
S'Ardia
Sedilo

August
Cursa a su Coccoi e Palio degli Asinelli a San Vito
Cursa to Coccoi and Palio of the Donkeys in San Vito
San Vito

Festa dei Candelieri
Feast of the Candlesticks
Sassari

Sagra della Mandorla
Almond Festival
Sinnai

September
Corsa degli Scalzi
Race of the Barefoot Runners
Cabras

October
La Sagra della Castagna e Dado
The Chestnut and Nut Festival
Aritzo

November
Sagra del Carciofo Samassi
The Artichoke Festival of Samassi
Samassi

The Creator made Italy from designs by Michelangelo
– Mark Twain

18

SICILIA

SICILY

Sicily is the largest island in the Mediterranean Sea and the hilly landscape is Italy's largest region in terms of land. Its coastline borders three seas: the Ionian, Tyrhennian, and Mediterranean. There are several islands included in this region: the Aeolian, the Aegadian, Pantelleria, and Lampedusa. Mount Etna is the tallest active volcano in Europe and dominates the eastern region of Sicily. Mount Etna is 2.5 times higher than Mount Vesuvius in Campania (outside of Naples), has snow during the winter months and even a ski area.

Earliest evidence of humans in Sicily dates back thousands of years. Before becoming part of Italy in 1860, Sicily was ruled by Aragon, Spain, Holy Roman Empire, Bourbons of Naples and the Kingdom of the Two Sicilies at different times. Ruins exist from the ancient tribes that inhabited the island, the Greek period, the Roman period and the middle ages. Several important archeologic sites exist on the island such as the Valley of the Temples, Selinunte, and the Necropolis at Pantalica. There are six UNESCO world heritage sites and three proposed sites on the island. Much of the population speak both Italian and Sicilian and live near Palermo and Catania.

Nicknamed "God's Kitchen" for the variety of wines and cuisine produced on the island, every area of Sicily has its own specialties. This region has the highest number of organic farmers in the country. The Sardinian diet is largely vegetables coupled with seafood. Pasta is a staple as with all of Southern Italy, as is rice, which is used in the typical *arancini* (rice balls fried in breadcrumbs). Couscous can be found in restaurants and on tables around the island, a legacy from its Arab-influenced heritage.

Sicilian desserts are not to be missed, including the gelato, cannoli, and biscotti. One of the most famous Italian dessert wines (also used for cooking) is Marsala. The Trapani province is the center of Marsala production. Sicily produces over 290 million gallons of wine a year, second only to Puglia, however, the Sicilians actually consume less wine per capita than other regions of Italy.

FESTIVAL FOCUS
Sagra del Mandorlo in Fiori
Feast of the Almond Blossoms
Agrigento

Agrigento was originally founded as a Greek colony in 581 BC and called Akragas. At various times it has been ruled by Byzantines, Romans and Arabs. The Greek presence is perhaps most felt at the Valle dei Tempi, home to five temple ruins that draw visitors from around the globe.

The Sagra del Mandorlo in Fiori celebrates the almonds of the area. Enjoy the parades and folk groups during this week-long celebration, in particular the Andalusian and Friesan horses included in some of the parades. Sicilian street food is served in Piazza Marconi but if you'd like something more formal, various restaurants participate in fixed menus that incorporate the use of the almond as the highlighted ingredient. If you are still eager for more local dancing and entertainment, an International Folklore Festival is held concurrently with Sagra del Mandorlo each year; two-for-one festival fun!

FESTIVALS OF SICILY

February
Carnevale di Acireale
Carnival of Acireale
Acireale

Sagra delle Mandorle in Fiore
Festival of Almond Blossom
Agrigento

Festa di Sant'Agata
Festival of Saint Agatha
Catania

April
Sagra del Carciofo
Artichoke Festival
Cerda

Sagra del Carfiofo
Artichoke Festival
Ramacca

May
Mattanza
Tuna Festival
Favignana

Mostra dei Formaggi della Vallee del Belice e Sagra della Ricotta
Vallee of the Belice Cheese Show and Festival of Ricotta
Poggioreale

June
Sagra della Ciliega
The Cherry Festival
Chiusa Sclafani

Inycon
Wine Festival
Menfi

Sagra del Cappero
Caper Festival
Pollara & Salina

July
Festa di Santa Rosalia
Festival of Saint Rosalia
Palermo

August
Sagra del Pesce
Fish Festival
Azzuro & Selinunte

Festa dei Burgisi e Sagra della Spiga a Gangi
Festival of Burgusu and Feast of the Ear of Gangi
Gangi

September
Sagra del Pistacchio
Pistachio Festival
Bronte

Sagra di Buon Riposo e Sagra della Salsiccia
Feast of the Good Rest and Sausage Festival
Calascibetta

Cous Cous Festa
Cous Cous Festival
San Vito Lo Capo

Festa di Sant'Antonio Abate
Feast of Sant'Antonio Abate
Santa Domenica Vittoria

October
Sagra del Carrubo
The Carob Festival
Frigintini

Sagra del Fico d'India
Prickly Pear Festival
Roccapalumba

Ottobrate Zafferanese
Zafferana October Festival
Zafferana Etnea

December
ChocoBarocco Modica - Quando il Cioccolato Incontra l'arte
ChocoBarocco Modica - When Chocolate Meets Art
Modica

Sagra della Ricotta
Ricotta Festival
Nardo

NOTES

Italy, and the Spring and first love all together should suffice to make the gloomiest person happy. – Bertrand Russell

19

TRENTINO-ALTO ADIGE

TRENTINO-SOUTH TYROL

A completely mountainous region, the Trentino-Alto Adige is quite literally a tale of two provinces. Trentino is the southern province and predominantly Italian-speaking; Alto Adige is the northern province, predominantly German-speaking and also known as Sud-Tirol or South Tyrol. It was formed in 1948 as a region and each of the provinces is autonomous. Trent is the capital of Trentino and Bolzano is the capital of Alto Adige. The region borders Austria and Switzerland and, until it was annexed from the Austro-Hungarian Empire after World War I, it was part of Austria, explaining the heavy influence on the cuisine and culture of the area. German-influenced dishes such as *Knödel* (dumplings) and *speck* (smoked bacon) are popular in the north and dishes with polenta and gnocchi are popular in the south. The region is home to many world class ski resorts.

The Trentino province is only about two hours from both Venice and Milan but doesn't garner the tourism that they do. Mushrooms, apples, grapes, plums, chestnuts, and olives are grown here. The town of San Michele all'Adige has the oldest wine making school in all of Italy. While this area is the northernmost olive oil producing region in the world, its mushrooms are the star attraction. In the capital of Trento there is a mushroom market on Piazza Ladron and each autumn complete with *Micologi*, mushroom experts/police that troll the stands to ensure that there aren't any poisonous mushrooms being sold. There is also a 700 year old fruit market in Bolzano at Piazza Erbe every day except Sunday.

Altoatesino is the Italian adjective used to describe the cuisine of this region. There are many types of cheeses made from the high altitude grazing cows of the region. Some of the cheeses have Italian names and some have German ones. Asiago, grana padano and provolone are three of the many varieties you have likely heard of. Speck Alto Adige is sliced so thin it practically melts in your mouth. With only 25 mass producers, two of which are approved for export to the United States, authentic speck can be difficult to find. It is quality controlled by the government and production takes about 22 weeks from start to finish. Other provincial specialties include *canderli* (dumplings) and Pane dei Francescani, an excellent bread made in the area.

FESTIVAL FOCUS
Festa del Formaggio
Festival of Cheese
Campo Tures

For one weekend in March, the market town of Campo Tures is a haven for *Turophiles*, connoisseurs and lovers of cheese, with three days full of exhibitions, talks, live cooking demonstrations and cheese tastings. There are five Protected Designation of Origin (DOP) quality-controlled cow's milk cheeses from this region: Asiago, Grana Padano, Provolone *Valpadana*, *Spressa delle Giudicarie*, and *Stelvio/Stilfser*. Approximately 100 cheese exhibitors from the Alto Adige region, other parts of Italy, and other countries exhibit close to 1,000 types of cheeses. Though the festival is only three days, restaurants in town will feature cheese tasting menus throughout the following week.

FESTIVALS OF TRENTINO-SOUTH TYROL

March
Mostra Vini Spumanti
Sparkling Wines Show
Madonna di Campiglio

Festa del Formaggio
Festival of Cheese
Campo Tures

April-May
Tempo di asparagi a Castelbello
Asparagus Time in Castelbello
Castelbello

Settimane degli Asparagi a Terlano
Asparagus Weeks in Terlano
Terlano

May
Festa degli Schützen a Bolzano
Festival of the Protectors in Bolzano
Bolzano

Rievocazione Storica del Voto di San Abbondio & Palio delle Botti
Historical Reenactment of the Vow of Saint Abbondio and Palio delle Botti
Dro

Festa della Mela
Apple Festival
Ora

Pane, vino e pesciolino
Bread, Wine & Fish
Riva del Garda

June
Feste Vigiliane
Parties of Borgo San Vigilio in the Historic Center of Trento
Trento

August
Festa del Latte
South Tyrolean Milk Festival
Malga Fane

September
Festa della Mela
Apple Festival
Caldonazzo

Festa dell'Uva
The Grape Festival
Verla di Giovo

October
Festa dell'Uva
The Grape Festival
Merano

La Desmontegada di Predazzo
The Return of Cows and Shepherds from Summer Pastures to Predazzo
Predazzo

October
Festa della Castagna
Chestnut Festival
Roncegno

Speck Festival
Speck Festival
Val di Funes

November
La Sagra della Ciuiga
The Festival of Ciuìga Sausage
San Lorenzo in Banale

20

TOSCANA

TUSCANY

Tuscany needs no introduction, famous the world over for its wines, food, hill towns, landscape, art, architecture and history, it is well-traveled and publicized. Often on itineraries for many visitors, Tuscany does not disappoint when it comes to food and folklore celebrations found throughout the region year-round. Like other regions, it has mountains for skiing, countryside for rambling, and beaches for lazing the day away.

The base of Tuscan cuisine is bread, legumes, and vegetables. Termed "rustic" and "*cucina povera*" (poor kitchen), Tuscan food is not lacking in any regard. A typical Tuscan meal may begin with small pieces of toasted bread, called crostini, served as appetizers with a variety of toppings accompanied by local salame. The first course may include the bread-based *ribolitta* soup or pasta served with wild boar or rabbit. Make sure you're hungry if you belly up to the table and order a *bistecca fiorentina*; this steak of gargantuan proportions deserves awe and respect. With a long Mediterranean coastline, the seafood soup called *cacciucco* is also a regional specialty. Desert may finish with some biscotti to dip in your *vin santo* wine or a piece of *castagnaccio* (chestnut cake). For something different, try a *semifreddo*; literally meaning "half cold" these desserts have a texture similar to a frozen mousse.

FESTIVAL FOCUS
Il Palio
The Race
Siena

While many folkloric traditions continue as a draw for both tradition and tourism, the Palio of Siena is by the Sienese for the Sienese. The Palio is held twice each year, on July 2 and August 16, but on the minds of every resident each day of the year. There are seventeen *contrade* (districts) and each is a community within a community of extended family with its own leaders, headquarters, flags, colors, museums, churches, patron saints, allies, and sworn enemies. The seventeen *contrade* are named Caterpiller, Conch Shell, Dragon, Elephant, Forest, Giraffe, Noble Goose, Leopard, Owl, Panther, Porcupine, Ram, She Wolf, Snail, Tortoise, Tower, Unicorn, and Wave.

Each *contrada* fields a *fantino* (jockey) and a horse for the race. Since space is limited and the course dangerous, only ten horses and fantinos run each race. The contrada selected to run will always be the seven that did not race the previous Palio and three additional selected through a lottery. They race to win the Palio, the unique, silken banner created for each race.

One month before each race the lots are drawn for which contrade will race. The week before the race, soil is brought in from the countryside to lay the dirt track over the cobblestones around Piazza del Campo. The main festivities start three days before each Palio when the horses for each contrada are selected; it is not until then that the contrade and fantinos know which horse their jockey will ride. The process looks a lot like bingo and kicks off the next part of the Palio precursor, strategy.

After it is known which horse each fantino will ride, the representatives for the contrades begin negotiating with each other. Horses and their jockeys are guarded by several members of the contrada to avoid foul play and contact with other contrade. Participating contrade will even go as far as paying another contrada to defeat its sworn enemy; some will try to bribe the jockeys. The days that follow include trial runs in the piazza, drummers, and flag bearers practicing and parading in the streets. The night before, hundreds of people sit at tables that seem to stretch on for miles in each contrada for dinner. Everyone is wearing their colors and passionately shouting the fight songs of their contrada.

On the day of the race, each horse is taken into the church of its respective contrada, sprinkled with holy water and blessed. About mid-afternoon a procession lasting several hours winds its way through the city and into Piazza del Campo. About 60,000 people are in the Campo waiting for the horse race to begin. The starting lineup is selected, they lineup at the starting line and once there are no false starts, they race to the finish whipping each other and their horses in an effort to gain position. The jockeys ride bareback through the dangerous course, which lasts about ninety seconds. It's the only horserace in the world where the horse wins the race, whether the rider is still on it or not.

In the end, everyone celebrates except the team that comes in second, they turn out their lights and become the quietest corner of the city. The August race is the most important but no less anxiety-ridden and exciting for anyone lucky enough to attend. Tickets can be hard to come by so plan well in advance or arrive very early to claim a spot inside the interior (where there are no facilities provided). If you arrive in Italy prior to the July Palio, you should also look into attending *Calcio Storico Fiorentino* in Florence held about eight days prior.

FESTIVALS OF TUSCANY

February
Carnevale di Viareggio
Carnival of Viareggio
Viareggio

March
Sagra del Tartufo Marzuolo
Marzuolo Truffle Fair
San Giovanni d'Asso

April
Scoppio del Carro
Exploding of the Cart at Easter
Florence

Marzolino, il Primo Pecorino
Marzolino - The First Pecorino Cheese
Pienza

Festa del Carciofo
Feast of Artichokes
Chisure
May

Sagra dei Pici
Pici Pasta Feast
Celle sul Rigo

Maggiolata Lucignano
May Festival
Lucignano

Serremaggio Serre di Rapolano
May Festival
Serre di Rapolano

Sagra del Fritto
Feast of Fried Foods
Monteroni d'Arbia

Sagra della Pastasciutta
Pastasciutta (Pasta) Festival
Siena

June
Giostre del Saracino (June)
Ride of the Saracens
Arezzo

Calcio Storico Fiorentino
Historical Florentine Soccer Match
Florence

Radda nel Bicchiere
Radda in the Glass
Radda in Chianti

Festa del Barabarossa
Feast of the Barbarossa
San Quirico d'Orcia

Gioco del Ponte
Game of the Bridge
Pisa

Sagra della Bistecca
Steak Festival
Serravalle Pistoiese

July
Monteriggioni di Torri si Corona Festa Medievale
Monteriggioni Crown Towers Medieval Festival
Monteriggioni

Feast Day of Saint James
Feast Day of Saint James
Pistoia

Corsa del Palio (July)
Palio Horse Race
Siena

August
Giostre del Saracino
Ride of the Saracens
Arezzo

Sagra del Pesce e Patate
Fish & Chips Festival
Barga

Sagra del Crostino
Crostini Feast
Castiglione d'Orcia

Sagra del Raviolo
Ravioli Feast
Contignano

Sagra del Polpo
Octopus Festival
Livorno

Sagra del Panigaccio
Festival of the Panigaccio
Podenzana

Corsa del Palio (August)
Palio Horse Race
Siena

September
Giostre del Saracino (September)
Ride of the Saracens
Arezzo

Sagra della Val d'Arbia
Feast of Val d'Arbia
Buonconvento

Sagra del Fico
Fig Festival
Carmignano

Rassegna del Chianti Classico Chianti
Classico Wine Festival
Greve in Chianti

Settimana del Miele
Week of Honey
Montalcino

Festa della Birra
Beer Festival
Buonconvento

October
Sagra del Marrone
Chestnut Fair
Campiglia d'Orcia

Sagra Del Tordo
Festival of the Thrush
Montalcino

Sagra del Fungo e della Castagna
Chestnut & Mushroom fair
Vivo d'Orcia

Festa del Galletto
Feast of the Cockerell
Camigliano

October - November
Mostra del Tartufo Bianco
White Truffle Fair
San Giovanni d'Asso

November
Sagra della Castagna
Chestnut fair
Piancastagnaio

December
Sagra dell'Olio
Olive Oil Festival
San Quirico d'Orcia

It's easy to understand why the most beautiful poems about England in the spring were written by poets living in Italy at the time. — Philip Dunne

21

UMBRIA

UMBRIA

Historical hill towns, rolling green hills, religious pilgrimages, black truffles, and chocolate; these are some of the many reasons why visitors choose to visit this region named after the Umbri people and often referred to as *"il cuore verde d'italia,"* the green heart of Italy. Landlocked by other Italian provinces, Umbria is classified as approximately 99% hills or mountains.

Umbria produces many famous products known throughout the word such as terra cotta pottery from Deruta, pasta by Buitoni, and chocolates by Perugina. An area of great natural beauty, there are beautiful mountain landscapes, national parks and gorgeous lakes to enjoy. Many Roman Catholics include Assisi on their Italian itineraries to pay homage to St. Francis of Assisi in his place of birth.

Traditional Umbrian cuisine highlights the produce and game of the region: black truffles, wild mushrooms, and wild boar (*cinghiale*). Black truffles are found mainly around Norcia and Spoleto. They are sniffed out by trained dogs or pigs and fetch a high price. The town of Norcia is also renowned for its cured meats and, in fact, top butchers in the area are called *norcinos*. Lentils from Castellucio are considered to be among the best in Italy and are used in soups and as *contorni* (side dishes). Umbria also produces fine wines and olive oil like its neighbor Tuscany.

FESTIVAL FOCUS
Corsa dei Ceri
Race of the Candles
Gubbio

Every May 15, teams from three different guilds participate in the challenge of carrying three very large, wooden candlesticks (*ceri*) on their shoulders through town and up a hill to the Basilica of Sant'Ubaldo. These giant-sized candlesticks are 13 feet tall and weigh in at over 800 pounds. The festivities actually begin well in advance; on the first Sunday in May, the ceri are accompanied by drummers and fanfare as they are carried horizontally into town from the Basilica where they are displayed since the previous year. The ceri are placed in the Arengo hall at the Palazzo dei Consoli until the 15th. On the eve of the 14th, everyone gathers at Piazza Grande to hear the *campanone* (large bell) rung at seven o'clock signifying the start of the competition the following day.

On the day of the race, drummers start beating their drums at 5:30 a.m. to wake the town officials and teams for each guild. At 6:00 the *campanone* rings again and at 7:00 there is a ceremony at the cemetery to honor past participants. At 8:00 there is a Catholic mass held and a child draws the name of the captains for the competition two years hence. Next there is a procession with Saints' statues followed by the 10:00 parade through the streets of Gubbio. After a series of enactments beginning at 11:30 the campanone rings and the ceri are raised to a vertical stance in Piazza Grande amongst a crowd of thousands and the *ceri* are walked through the town vertically on display to await the Bishop's blessing and the beginning of the race at 6:00 p.m. The ceri are finally raced through the town and up the hillside over 2.6 miles back to the Basilica. It's a very long day filled with ceremony and fanfare that has endured for centuries.

FESTIVALS OF UMBRIA

February
Nero Norcia
Black Truffles of Norcia
Norcia

Festa dell'Olivo/Sagre della Bruschetta
Festival of Olive Oil and Bruschetta
Spello

April
Coloriamo i Cieli
Kite Festival
Castiglione del Lago

Settimana Enologica
Wine Week
Montefalco

Corsa all'Anello
The Ring Race
Narni

May
Festa del Calendimaggio
The May Day Festival
Assisi

Corsa dei Ceri
Race of the Candlesticks
Gubbio

Palio della Balestra
Crossbow Contest
Gubbio

Cantamaggio
Cantamaggio
Terni

June
Festa del Voto
Festival of the Vote
Assisi

Festa della Ciliegia
The Cherry Festival
Bazzano

Mercato delle Gaite
Medieval Market of Gaite
Bevagna

Festa della Fioritura
Festival of the Flowers
Castellucio di Norcia

Giostra della Quintana
Joust of the Quintana
Foligno

Festa delle Acque
Festival of Water
Piediluco

July
Palio delle Barche (Festival of Boats)
Palio of the Boats (Festival of Boats)
Passignano sul Trasimeno

Sagra del Prosciutto e Melone
Feast of Prosciutto and Melon
Villastrada

August
Palio di San Rufino
Palio di San Rufino
Assisi

Palio dei Terzieri
Palio dei Terzieri
Citta della Pieve

Palio dei Quartieri
Contest of the Districts
Nocera Umbra

September
Giostra della Quintana
Joust of the Quintana
Foligno

Giochi delle Porte
Games of the Doors
Gualdo Tadino

Festa dell'Uva
Festival of the Grape
Montefalco
September

Calvalcata di Satriano
The Ride of Satriano
Nocera Umbra

Giostra dell'Arme di San Gemini
Joust of Saint Gemini
San Gemini

October
Mostra del Tartufo
Truffle Show
Citta del Castello

Festival Eurochocolate
Festival Eurochocolate
Perugia

Ottobre Trevano
Trevi October Festival
Trevi

Palio dei Terzieri
Palio dei Terzieri
Trevi

November
Fiera dei Morti
Fair of the Dead
Pian di Massiano

Venice is like eating and entire box of chocolate liqueurs in one go.
— Truman Capote

22

VENETO

VENETO

Home to more than just the famous city of Venice in its coastal territory, Veneto has great geological diversity with an alpine mountain zone bordering Austria, a hill zone, and plains. The geography produces a diverse line of specialty cuisines. In this region you are more likely to find rice and polenta as staples than pasta. Food highlights include fish of the Adriatic Sea, the white asparagus of Bassano, radicchio from Treviso, and asiago from the Vicenza province.

Venice is a "must-do" on everyone's first trip to Italy, and it was once the center of the world's spice trade. There is much to explore in the Veneto region. Verona is home to a world famous opera festival, the largest wine expo (Vinitaly) and of course, Romeo and Juliet. Cortina d'Ampezzo offers world class skiing. Beaches dot the coast along the Adriatic Sea. Grappa and asiago cheese are produced in Vicenza. Strolling the lakeside in Bardolino on the eastern shore of Lake Garda is popular. There are seventeen DOC wine zones in the Veneto, and *Valpolicella* and *Amarone* are two well-known exports. The Amarone is a rich, powerful red and Valpolicella is the light, fragrant red table wine.

Asiago cheese production in the alpine/sub-alpine area of the region has a DOP seal, government-inspected quality. The Consorzio Tutela Formaggio Asiago based in Vicenza regulates and oversees all of the production of the cheese, from where the cows are grazing, to how the cheese is made and through its production. It is aged up to three years on wooden shelves and turned every single day by hand both as part of the process and for quality control observation. There are five levels of aged asiago: *fresco* (up to 40 days); *allevo* or *stragionato* (more than 60 days); *mezzano* (4-6 months); *vecchio* (more than 10 months); *stravecchio* (more than 15 months). It takes two million gallons of milk to make 25,000 wheels of asiago.

FESTIVAL FOCUS
Festa del Redentore
Feast of the Redeemer
Venice

The Feast of the Redeemer was first celebrated in 1575 to mark the end of a plague on the city. It is held each July 19 and the government sets up a temporary pontoon bridge to handle the crowds of people flocking to the church of Il Redentore across the canal on the Venetian island of Giudecca.

This festival is so important to the Venetians that in 1717 Handel composed his Water Music just for this event and it continues to be played from small rafts positioned in the lagoon. At night every inch of the Grand Canal is lined with people preparing to see a spectacular display of fireworks reflected in the lagoon and canals. Many people who live on the canal line the docksides with tables and eat a traditional meal of stuffed duck or fried Adriatic sole with friends and family before the fireworks display begins.

FESTIVALS OF THE VENETO

February
Carnevale di Venezia
Carnival of Venice
Venice

Bacanal del Gnoco Carnevale
Bacchanal of Gnoco Carnival
Verona

March
Su e Zo per i Ponti
Up & Down Over the Bridges Race
Venice

April
Sagra dell'Asparago di Bassano
White Asparagus Festival
Bassano del Grappo

Festa di San Marco
Feast of Saint Mark
Venice

May
Festa degli Asparagi
Asparagus Festival
Cavaion

Festa dea Sparesea
Aspargus Goddess Festival
Cavallino

May
Valpollicellore
Valpolicella Wine Celebration
Illasi

Festa della Sensa
Festival of the Sensa
Venice

Festa Medioevale del vino Soave Bianco Soave
Medieval Festival with Soave White Wine
Venice

Vogalonga
The Long Row
Venice

June
Sagra di San Pietro di Castello
San Pietro di Castello Festival
Venice

July
Sardellata al Pal del Vo
Sardellata at Pal del Vo
Pal de Vo

Festa del Redentore
Feast of the Redeemer
Venice

August
Palio di Feltre
Palio of Feltre
Feltre

September
Sagra del Pesce di Burano
Burano Fish Festival
Burano

Partita a Scacchi
Giant Chess Match
Marostica

Palio dei Dieci Comuni
Palio of the Ten Towns
Montagnana

Regata Storica
Historical Regatta
Venice

October
Festa dell'Uva
Bardolino Grape Festival
Bardolino

Festa del Mosto
Feast of the Must (grapes)
Sant'Erasmo

November
Festa del Vino Novello
Feast of New Wine
Bardolino

Festa della Madonna della Salute
Festival of the Madonna
Venice

Festa di San Martino
Feast of San Martino
Venice

December
Festa del Radicchio
Radicchio Festival
Asigliano

NOTES

GLOSSARY

English	Italian
almond	*mandorla*
anchovy	*acciuga*
appetizer	*aperitivo*
apple	*mela*
apricot	*albicocca*
artichoke	*carciofo*
asparagus	*asparago*
bean	*fagiolo*
beef	*manzo*
bread	*pane*
bruschetta	*bruschetta*
calzone	*calzone*
capers	*capperi*
carnival	*carnevale*
cauliflower	*cavolfiore*
cheese	*formaggio*
cherry	*ciliegia*
chestnut	*castagna*
chickpea	*cece*
chile pepper	*peperoncino*
chocolate	*cioccolato*
corn	*mais*
couscous	*couscous*
dinner	*cena*
duck	*anatra*
feast	*festa, sagra*

festival	*sagra, festival*
fig	*fichi*
fish	*pesce*
flowers	*fiori*
focaccia	*focaccia*
frog	*rana*
garlic	*aglio*
grape	*uva*
honey	*miele*
lamb	*agnello*
lard	*lardo*
lemon	*limone*
lentils	*lenticchie*
lunch	*pranzo*
melon	*melone*
milk	*latte*
mushroom	*fungo*
octopus	*polipo*
olive oil	*olio d'oliva*
onion	*cipolla*
party	*festa*
pasta	*pasta*
peach	*pesca*
pear	*pera*
peppers	*peperoni*
pistachio	*pistacchio*
pizza	*pizza*
polenta	*polenta*
pork	*maiale*
potato	*patata*

prickly pear	*fico d'india*
prosciutto	*prosciutto*
pumpkin	*zucca*
rabbit	*coniglio*
radicchio	*raddicchio*
ricotta	*ricotta*
risotto	*risotto*
salami	*salame*
sausage	*salsiccia*
seafood	*frutti di mare*
snails	*lumache*
soup	*la minestra*
speck	*granello*
strawberry	*fragola*
sweets	*dolci*
sword fish	*pesce spada*
tomato	*pomodoro*
truffles	*tartufi*
turkey	*tacchino*
wine	*vino*

GLOSSARY

Italiano	Inglese
acciuga	anchovy
aglio	garlic
agnello	lamb
albicocca	apricot
anatra	duck
aperitivo	appetizer
asparago	asparagus
bruschetta	bruschetta
calzone	calzone
capperi	capers
carciofo	artichoke
carnevale	carnival
castagna	chestnut
cavolfiore	cauliflower
cece	chickpea
ciliegia	cherry
cena	dinner
cioccolato	chocolate
cipolla	onion
coniglio	rabbit
couscous	couscous
dolci	sweets
fagiolo	bean
festa	party, feast
festival	festival
fichi	fig

fico d'india	*prickly pear*
fiori	*flowers*
focaccia	*focaccia*
formaggio	*cheese*
fragola	*strawberry*
frutti di mare	*seafood*
fungo	*mushroom*
granello	*speck*
la minestra	*soup*
lardo	*lard*
latte	*milk*
lenticchie	*lentils*
limone	*lemon*
lumache	*snails*
maiale	*pork*
mais	*corn*
mandorla	*almond*
manzo	*beef*
mela	*apple*
melone	*melon*
miele	*honey*
olio d'oliva	*olive oil*
pane	*bread*
pasta	*pasta*
patata	*potato*
peperoncino	*chile pepper*
peperoni	*peppers*
pera	*pear*
pesca	*peach*
pesce	*fish*

pesce spada	*sword fish*
pistacchio	*pistachio*
pizza	*pizza*
polenta	*polenta*
polipo	*octopus*
pomodoro	*tomato*
pranzo	*lunch*
prosciutto	*prosciutto*
radicchio	*raddicchio*
rana	*frog*
ricotta	*ricotta*
risotto	*risotto*
sagra	*festival, feast*
salame	*salami*
salsiccia	*sausage*
tacchino	*turkey*
tartufi	*truffles*
uva	*grape*
vino	*wine*
zucca	*pumpkin*

FOOD FESTIVAL CROSS-REFERENCE

Food	Page
almond	111, 116
anchovy	79
appetizer	41, 134
apple	23, 66, 125
apricot	47
artichoke	14, 46, 70, 90, 112, 116, 132
asparagus	55, 65, 70, 84, 102, 124, 148, 149
bean	18, 35
beef	133
beer	135
bread	23, 55, 91, 125
bruschetta	69, 140
calzone	65
capers	117
carnival	27, 54, 69, 83, 90, 110, 116, 131, 148
cauliflower	69
cheese	17, 23, 29, 35, 47, 48, 57, 59, 65, 85, 104, 117, 119, 124, 131
cherry	46, 117, 141
chestnut	24, 36, 42, 49, 58, 72, 112, 126, 136

ABOUT THE AUTHOR

Lisa Vogele is a self-described Italophile, festival-lover, and travel-addict. Her travel blog Lisa Loves to Travel has been created to share her love of festivals with fellow travelers and enthusiasts (www.lisalovestotravel.com). The "Food & Folklore" series is published by Lisa's Travel Guides and highlights food, fun, and festivals to help others go local as a traveler, not a tourist.

Lisa loves hearing about your experiences, suggestions, and recommendations about festival travel. She can be contacted via email at lisa@lisastravelguides.com or follow her on Twitter @travelwithlisa. For information about forthcoming books in the Food & Folklore series check out www.lisastravelguides.com.

Originally from Connecticut, Lisa and her husband Mark call the beautiful mountains of Colorado home.

ABOUT THIS BOOK

FOOD & FOLKLORE   A Year of Italian Festivals
1st Edition
ISBN: 0692722432 / ISBN-13: 978-0692722435
First published in 2016
Copyright 2016 © Lisa M. Vogele

LISA'S TRAVEL GUIDES
Lisa M. Vogele
PO Box 5257
Snowmass Village, Colorado 81615
USA
www.lisastravelguides.com

Cover design by Ad Vogele
Author photo by: Robin Russo
All other photos by: Lisa M. Vogele
Blue door on cover by: collectmoments on Flickr:
https://www.flickr.com/photos/collectmoments/7850562934/collectmoments on Flickr
Map by d-maps.com
http://d-maps.com/carte.php?num_car=18137&lang=en

NOTES

NOTES

NOTES

NOTES

NOTES